Drug Trafficking

Other Books in the Current Controversies Series

CONTROVERSIES

Drug Trafficking

Julia Bauder, Book Editor

GREENHAVEN PRESS

An imprint of Thomson Gale, a part of The Thomson Corporation

Detroit • New York • San Francisco • New Haven, Conn. • Waterville, Maine • London

THOMSON
GALE

Christine Nasso, *Publisher*
Elizabeth Des Chenes, *Managing Editor*

© 2008 The Gale Group.

Star logo is a trademark and Gale and Greenhaven Press are registered trademarks used herein under license.

For more information, contact:
Greenhaven Press
27500 Drake Rd.
Farmington Hills, MI 48331-3535
Or you can visit our Internet site at http://www.gale.com

Articles in Greenhaven Press anthologies are often edited for length to meet page require-ments. In addition, original titles of these works are changed to clearly present the main thesis and to explicitly indicate the author's opinion. Every effort is made to ensure that Greenhaven Press accurately reflects the original intent of the authors. Every effort has been made to trace the owners of copyrighted material.

ISBN-13: 978-0-7377-3281-8 (hardcover)
ISBN-10: 0-7377-3281-4 (hardcover)
ISBN-13: 978-0-7377-3282-5 (pbk.)
ISBN-10: 0-7377-3282-2 (pbk.)

Library of Congress Control Number: 2007937459

Contents

Chapter 2: Are Efforts to Stop Drug Trafficking Harming the United States?

A Florida man was sent to jail for twenty-five years for drug trafficking, even though he was not selling drugs. The man was simply trying to acquire legal prescription drugs to treat his severe back pain.

**No: The War on Drugs Is a
Reasonable Response to the Dangers
of Drug Trafficking**

Chapter 4: Are Efforts to Stop Drug Trafficking Helping the War on Terror?

Foreword

By definition, controversies are "discussions of questions in which opposing opinions clash" (Webster's Twentieth Century Dictionary Unabridged). Few would deny that controversies are a pervasive part of the human condition and exist on virtually every level of human enterprise. Controversies transpire between individuals and among groups, within nations and between nations. Controversies supply the grist necessary for progress by providing challenges and challengers to the status quo. They also create atmospheres where strife and warfare can flourish. A world without controversies would be a peaceful world; but it also would be, by and large, static and prosaic.

The Series' Purpose

The purpose of the Current Controversies series is to explore many of the social, political, and economic controversies dominating the national and international scenes today. Titles selected for inclusion in the series are highly focused and specific. For example, from the larger category of criminal justice, Current Controversies deals with specific topics such as police brutality, gun control, white collar crime, and others. The debates in Current Controversies also are presented in a useful, timeless fashion. Articles and book excerpts included in each title are selected if they contribute valuable, long-range ideas to the overall debate. And wherever possible, current information is enhanced with historical documents and other relevant materials. Thus, while individual titles are current in focus, every effort is made to ensure that they will not become quickly outdated. Books in the Current Controversies series will remain important resources for librarians, teachers, and students for many years.

In addition to keeping the titles focused and specific, great care is taken in the editorial format of each book in the series. Book introductions and chapter prefaces are offered to provide background material for readers. Chapters are organized around several key questions that are answered with diverse opinions representing all points on the political spectrum. Materials in each chapter include opinions in which authors clearly disagree as well as alternative opinions in which authors may agree on a broader issue but disagree on the possible solutions. In this way, the content of each volume in Current Controversies mirrors the mosaic of opinions encountered in society. Readers will quickly realize that there are many viable answers to these complex issues. By questioning each author's conclusions, students and casual readers can begin to develop the critical thinking skills so important to evaluating opinionated material.

Current Controversies is also ideal for controlled research. Each anthology in the series is composed of primary sources taken from a wide gamut of informational categories including periodicals, newspapers, books, U.S. and foreign government documents, and the publications of private and public organizations. Readers will find factual support for reports, debates, and research papers covering all areas of important issues. In addition, an annotated table of contents, an index, a book and periodical bibliography, and a list of organizations to contact are included in each book to expedite further research.

Perhaps more than ever before in history, people are confronted with diverse and contradictory information. During the Persian Gulf War, for example, the public was not only treated to minute-to-minute coverage of the war, it was also inundated with critiques of the coverage and countless analyses of the factors motivating U.S. involvement. Being able to sort through the plethora of opinions accompanying today's major issues, and to draw one's own conclusions, can be a complicated and frustrating struggle. It is the editors' hope that Current Controversies will help readers with this struggle.

Introduction

Drug trafficking is undeniably a violent business. Many people have become numb to the everyday violence of drug trafficking—the murders, assaults, and other violent crimes that plague most large American cities and that are frequently traced back to the drug business—but some stories of drug-related violence retain their power to shock. Two such stories are those of Angela Dawson and Mario Núñez Magaña.

Dawson used to live in Baltimore, Maryland, with her husband, Carnell, and five of her six children. Baltimore has one of the worst drug problems in the United States: By some estimates 10 percent of the adults in the city are addicted to drugs, and Baltimore consistently has one of the country's highest murder rates. Dawson, like many people in Baltimore, did not appreciate the drug dealers who liked to stand on the corner by her house selling drugs and making trouble, but unlike most people Dawson decided to do something about it. She called the police every few days to report crimes, and she would even go outside and tell the drug dealers to go away.

The drug dealers in Dawson's area did not appreciate her interference. They retaliated by writing graffiti on Dawson's wall and throwing bricks through her windows. On October 2, 2002, the drug dealers stepped up their campaign against the Dawsons by throwing a Molotov cocktail [a bottle filled with gasoline] through their kitchen window. Dawson put out the fire by pouring water on it, and the family remained in the house.

Two weeks later, the drug dealers tried again to burn down the Dawsons' house. This time they succeeded. Early in the morning on October 16, a young man who lived across the street from the Dawsons broke down their front door, poured gasoline around the first floor, and lit it on fire. Angela and Carnell Dawson and their five children, ages nine to fourteen were all killed.

In Acapulco, Mexico, Núñez Magaña also tried to take on drug traffickers, and he also paid for it with his life. The thirty-five-year-old Magaña was the commander of a rapid-response antidrug team that was part of Mexico's federal Preventative Police. In March 2006 this team fought a gun battle with a group of drug traffickers outside of a federal building in Acapulco. Four of the drug traffickers were killed. The next month the drug traffickers responded by decapitating Núñez Magaña and another member of his team, jamming their heads onto a fence in front of the federal building where the gunfight occurred, and taping a note under the heads that read, "So you will learn to respect."

Even though drug-trafficking-related violence is condemned by essentially everyone who is not involved in the drug trade, there is much less agreement over how to deal with the problem. Should drug traffickers be given harsher prison sentences? Should people who use drugs be treated for their addictions so that there will be fewer drug buyers and less money going to drug traffickers? Should governments try to cut down on the supply of drugs by seizing drug shipments and paying foreign farmers not to grow drugs? Should drugs be legalized and their production and distribution handed over to legitimate pharmaceutical companies? These are some of the questions debated by the authors in *Current Controversies: Drug Trafficking*.

CHAPTER 1

Can Drug Trafficking Be Stopped?

Chapter Preface

The scale of the drug trafficking industry is a hard thing to measure. Even in the legal economy, it is extremely difficult to tally up all of the millions of small transactions that go into the making and selling of a particular product. With drugs—whose manufacturers and dealers do not generally respond to surveys or file reports with the Internal Revenue Service or the Securities and Exchange Commission—it is impossible.

The impossibility of measuring drug trafficking accurately is one of the factors that has boosted the popularity of news stories about record-breaking drug busts. Such stories have appeared frequently in the media in recent years. In May 2005 what was billed as the largest-ever drug bust in the world occurred when just shy of fourteen tons of cocaine were seized by Colombian police. (In reality, despite the media hype, that was not the biggest drug bust in terms of pounds seized; that record is held by a 1989 bust in Sylmar, California, when agents found 23.5 tons of cocaine stored in a warehouse.) Another record-breaking bust, which the media declared to be the largest-ever drug bust at sea, happened in May 2001 when the U.S. Coast Guard seized a ship carrying over thirteen tons of cocaine. That record was surpassed in March 2007, when twenty-one tons of cocaine were seized by the U.S. Coast Guard off Panama.

Two types of commentary tend to accompany the news of these record-breaking busts. On the one side, some people argue that such busts are evidence that the War on Drugs is working. Clearly, these people say, when the authorities take such large quantities of drugs out of circulation that must result in a lower quantity of drugs on American streets, at least temporarily. Others, taking a more pessimistic view, say that giant drug busts prove that the War on Drugs is not succeeding at reducing drug trafficking. After all, they note, assembling a multiton stash of cocaine is not an easy process, and the fact that there are still drug cartels that are large enough, well-financed enough, and well-organized enough to do so shows that the War on Drugs has not done a great deal of harm to those cartels.

As long as firm information about the extent of drug trafficking remains, arguments such as these will continue. The authors in this chapter join this debate over whether the War on Drugs is a winning or a losing battle.

A Balanced Antidrug Strategy Can Stop Drug Trafficking

Drug Enforcement Administration

The Drug Enforcement Administration is a U.S. government agency that enforces federal laws against the production and trafficking of drugs.

We have made significant progress in fighting drug use and drug trafficking in America. Now is not the time to abandon our efforts.

- Legalization advocates claim that the fight against drugs has not been won and is, in fact, unconquerable. They frequently state that people still take drugs, drugs are widely available, and that efforts to change this are futile. They contend that legalization is the only workable alternative.

Demand Reduction

- The facts are to the contrary to such pessimism. On the demand side, the U.S. has reduced casual use, chronic use and addiction, and prevented others from even starting using drugs. Overall drug use in the United States is down by more than a third since the late 1970s. That's 9.5 miilion people fewer using illegal drugs. We've reduced cocaine use by an astounding 70% during the last 15 years. That's 4.1 million fewer people using cocaine.

- Almost two-thirds of teens say their schools are drug-free, according to a new survey of teen drug use conducted by The National Center on Addiction and Sub-

Drug Enforcement Administration, *Speaking Out Against Drug Legalization*, U.S. Department of Justice, May 2003, pp. 4–7.

stance Abuse (CASA) at Columbia University. This is the first time in the seven-year history of the study that a majority of public school students report drug-free schools.

- The good news continues. According to the 2001–2002 PRIDE [Parents' Resource Institute for Drug Education] survey [mandated by federal law as an official measurement of adolescent drug use in America since 1998], student drug use has reached the lowest level in nine years. According to the author of the study, "following 9/11, Americans seemed to refocus on family, community, spirituality, and nation." These statistics show that U.S. efforts to educate kids about the dangers of drugs are making an impact. Like smoking cigarettes, drug use is gaining a stigma which is the best cure for this problem, as it was in the 1980s, when government, business, the media and other national institutions came together to do something about the growing problem of drugs and drug-related violence. This is a trend we should encourage—not send the opposite message of greater acceptance of drug use.

- The crack cocaine epidemic of the 1980s and early 1990s has diminished greatly in scope. And we've reduced the number of chronic heroin users over the last decade. In addition, the number of new marijuana users and cocaine users continues to steadily decrease.

- The number of new heroin users dropped from 156,000 in 1976 to 104,000 in 1999, a reduction of 33 percent.

- Of course, drug policy also has an impact on general crime. In a 2001 study, the British Home Office found violent crime and property crime increased in the late 1990s in every wealthy country except the United

States. Our murder rate is too high, and we have much to learn from those with greater success—but this reduction is due in part to a reduction in drug use.

- There is still much progress to make. There are still far too many people using cocaine, heroin and other illegal drugs. In addition, there are emerging drug threats like Ectasy and methamphetamine. But the fact is that our current policies balancing prevention, enforcement, and treatment have kept drug usage outside the scope of acceptable behavior in the U.S.

- To put things in perspective, less than 5 percent of the population uses illegal drugs of any kind. Think about that: More than 95 percent of Americans do not use drugs. How could anyone but the most hardened pessimist call this a losing struggle?

Less potent and deadly drugs are hitting the streets, and dealers are making less profits.

Supply Reduction

- There have been many successes on the supply side of the drug fight, as well. For example, Customs officials have made major seizures along the U.S.-Mexico border during a six-month period after September 11th [2001] seizing almost twice as much as the same period in 2001. At one port in Texas, seizures of methamphetamine are up 425% and heroin by 172%. Enforcement makes a difference—traffickers' costs go up with these kinds of seizures.

- Purity levels of Colombian cocaine are declining too, according to an analysis of samples seized from traffickers and bought from street dealers in the United States. The purity has declined by nine percent, from

86 percent in 1998, to 78 percent in 2001. There are a number of possible reasons for this decline in purity, including DEA [Drug Enforcement Administration] supply reduction efforts in South America.

- One DEA program, Operation Purple, involves 28 countries and targets the illegal diversion of chemicals used in processing cocaine and other illicit drugs. DEA's labs have discovered that the oxidation levels for cocaine have been greatly reduced, suggesting that Operation Purple is having a detrimental impact on the production of cocaine.

- Another likely cause is that traffickers are diluting their cocaine to offset the higher costs associated with payoffs to insurgent and paramilitary groups in Colombia. The third possible cause is that cocaine traffickers simply don't have the product to simultaneously satisfy their market in the United States and their rapidly growing market in Europe. As a result, they are cutting the product to try to satisfy both.

- Whatever the final reasons for the decline in drug purity, it is good news for the American public. It means less potent and deadly drugs are hitting the streets, and dealers are making less profits—that is, unless they raise their own prices, which helps price more and more Americans out of the market.

- Purity levels have also been reduced on methamphetamine by controls on chemicals necessary for its manufacture. The average purity of seized methamphetamine samples dropped from 72 percent in 1994 to 40 percent in 2001.

- The trafficking organizations that sell drugs are finding that their profession has become a lot more costly. In the mid-1990s, the DEA helped dismantle Burma's

Shan United Army, at the time the world's largest heroin trafficking organization, which in two years helped reduce the amount of Southeast Asian heroin in the United States from 63 percent of the market to 17 percent of the market. In the mid-1990s, the DEA helped disrupt the Cali cartel, which had been responsible for much of the world's cocaine.

- Progress does not come overnight. America has had a long, dark struggle with drugs. It's not a war we've been fighting for 20 years. We've been fighting it for 120 years. In 1880, many drugs, including opium and cocaine, were legal. We didn't know their harms, but we soon learned. We saw the highest level of drug use ever in our nation, per capita. There were over 400,000 opium addicts in our nation. That's twice as many per capita as there are today. And like today, we saw rising crime with that drug abuse. But we fought those problems by passing and enforcing tough laws and by educating the public about the dangers of these drugs. And this vigilance worked—by World War II, drug use was reduced to the very margins of society. And that's just where we want to keep it. With a 95 percent success rate—bolstered by an effective, three-pronged strategy combining education/prevention, enforcement, and treatment—we shouldn't give up now.

A Balanced Approach

A balanced approach of prevention, enforcement, and treatment is the key in the fight against drugs.

- Over the years, some people have advocated a policy that focuses narrowly on controlling the supply of drugs. Others have said that society should rely on treatment alone. Still others say that prevention is the only viable solution. As the 2002 National Drug Strategy observes, "What the nation needs is an honest effort to integrate these strategies."

- Drug treatment courts are a good example of this new balanced approach to fighting drug abuse and addiction in this country. These courts are given a special responsibility to handle cases involving drug-addicted offenders through an extensive supervision and treatment program. Drug court programs use the varied experience and skills of a wide variety of law enforcement and treatment professionals: judges, prosecutors, defense counsels, substance abuse treatment specialists, probation officers, law enforcement and correctional personnel, educational and vocational experts, community leaders and others—all focused on one goal: to help cure addicts of their addiction, and to keep them cured.

- Drug treatment courts are working. Researchers estimate that more than 50 percent of defendants convicted of drug possession will return to criminal behavior within two to three years. Those who graduate from drug treatment courts have far lower rates of recidivism, ranging from 2 to 20 percent. That's very impressive when you consider that for addicts who enter a treatment program voluntarily, 80 to 90 percent leave by the end of the first year. Among such dropouts, relapse within a year is generally the rule.

- What makes drug treatment courts so different? Graduates are held accountable for sticking with the program. Unlike other, purely voluntary treatment programs, the addict—who has a physical need for drugs—can't simply quit treatment whenever he or she feels like it.

- Law enforcement plays an important role in the drug treatment court program. It is especially important in the beginning of the process because it often triggers treatment for people who need it. Most people do not volunteer for drug treatment. It is more often an out-side motivator, like an arrest, that gets—and keeps—people in treatment. And it is important for judges to keep people in incarceration if treatment fails.

• There are already more than 123,000 people who use heroin at least once a month, and 1.7 million who use cocaine at least once a month. For them, treatment is the answer. But for most Americans, particularly the young, the solution lies in prevention, which in turn is largely a matter of education and enforcement, which aims at keeping drug pushers away from children and teenagers.

• The role of strong drug enforcement has been analyzed by R.E. Peterson. He has broken down the past four decades into two periods. The first period, from 1960 to 1980, was an era of permissive drug laws. During this era, drug incarceration rates fell almost 80 percent. Drug use among teens, meanwhile, climbed by more than 500 percent. The second period, from 1980 to 1995, was an era of stronger drug laws. During this era, drug use by teens dropped by more than a third.

The element of risk, created by strong drug enforcement policies, raises the price of drugs, and therefore lowers the demand.

Enforcing Laws Lowers Demand

• Enforcement of our laws creates risks that discourage drug use. Charles Van Deventer, a young writer in Los Angeles, wrote about this phenomenon in an article in *Newsweek*. He said that from his experience as a casual user—and he believes his experience with illegal drugs is "by far the most common"—drugs aren't nearly as easy to buy as some critics would like people to believe. Being illegal, they are too expensive, their quality is too unpredictable, and their purchase entails too many risks. "The more barriers there are," he said, "be they the cops or the hassle or the fear of dying, the less likely you are to get addicted. . . . The road to addiction was just bumpy enough," he concluded, "that I chose not to go down it. In this sense, we are winning the war on drugs just by fighting them."

- The element of risk, created by strong drug enforcement policies, raises the price of drugs, and therefore lowers the demand. A research paper, *Marijuana and Youth* funded by the Robert Wood Johnson Foundation, concludes that changes in the price of marijuana "contributed significantly to the trends in youth marijuana use between 1982 and 1998, particularly during the contraction in use from 1982 to 1992." That contraction was a product of many factors, including a concerted effort among federal agencies to disrupt domestic production and distribution; these factors contributed to a doubling of the street price of marijuana in the space of a year.

- The 2002 National Drug Control Strategy states that drug control policy has just two elements: modifying individual behavior to discourage and reduce drug use and addiction, and disrupting the market for illegal drugs. Those two elements call for a balanced approach to drug control, one that uses prevention, enforcement, and treatment in a coordinated policy. This is a simple strategy and an effective one. The enforcement side of the fight against drugs, then, is an integrated part of the overall strategy.

The U.S.'s Andean Counterdrug Initiative Is Reducing Drug Production in Latin America

Robert B. Charles

Robert B. Charles is the former U.S. assistant secretary of state for international narcotics and law enforcement affairs.

Thank you for the invitation to discuss the Andean Counterdrug Initiative (ACI) and the State Department's continued efforts in this critical region. The Initiative represents a significant investment by the American people in a region that produces the vast majority of the drugs arriving in the United States.

If this initiative were targeted just at saving some of the 21,000 lives lost to these drugs last year, it would be the right thing to do. But there is more to this bipartisan, multi-year initiative than even that noble aim. It is also a bulwark against the threat of terrorism in Colombia, Bolivia, Peru, Brazil, Venezuela, Ecuador, and Panama. In short, it is a regional hemispheric and national security program, with direct implications, for homeland security and for our well being here in the continental United States. One need only look as far as Haiti to see that drug money, and the instability that follows it, can be institutionally corrosive, to the point of breakdown. In Colombia and elsewhere in the hemisphere, the link between drug money and terrorism is incontrovertible.

All of this reinforces the wisdom of Congress in empowering the State Department, and the Bureau of International Narcotics and Law Enforcement (INL) in particular, to protect

Robert B. Charles, "U.S. Policy and the Andean Counterdrug Initiative (ACI), Testimony to the U.S. House Government Reform Committee, Subcommittee on Criminal Justice, Drug Policy, and Human Resources," www.state.gov, *Bureau of International Narcotics and Law Enforcement Affairs*, March 2, 2004.

Americans and our allies in this hemisphere by strengthening the rule of law, building law enforcement and justice sector capacity, cultivating non-drug sources of income, and stopping heroin and cocaine from being produced and shipped to our shores.

In the future, as in the past, strong congressional support will be critical to fully achieving the endgame. The endgame is a hemisphere in which drug-funded terrorism, corruption of struggling democracies by drug traffickers along with drug violence and drug abuse from the streets of Bogotá, [Colombia] to the streets of Baltimore, are reduced dramatically. We are making real progress toward that end state, and the Andean Counterdrug initiative is a major part of that palpable progress. . . .

The investment we have made is bearing fruit—drug production is down, traffickers are being arrested and extradited, legitimate jobs created, and the rule of law expanded. Our security, development, and institutional assistance to the judicial and law enforcement sectors are having a positive impact. The job is only half done, but the results are coming in and we are approaching what may well be a tipping point.

Antidrug Efforts in Colombia

The strategic centerpiece of the Andean Counterdrug Initiative (ACI) is INL programming in Colombia, the source of 90 percent of all the cocaine reaching the United States. Colombia also provides upwards to 70 percent of the heroin reaching our streets, and it also is a leading supplier of cocaine to Brazil, Europe, and points East. Besides being a producer of raw materials for cocaine and heroin, Colombia is a major manufacturer of refined drugs. And it is the world headquarters for major criminal and narco-terrorist organizations. What we do in Colombia affects us in United States, but also affects regional security and the growth of economic opportunities for those who wish to live in democracies free from drugs and terror.

Over the past two years, long awaited ACI funds have hit the ground, and they are making a difference. With INL support, the Colombian Government has eradicated both coca and heroin poppy at a pace that should begin to seriously deter future growing, even as it wipes out larger and larger percentages of the crops that currently become cocaine and heroin. The physical risks associated with this program have been great, but the strategy is proving both successful and justified. The Colombians and we have lost assets as well as personnel to the enemy. Three hostages, who are still in Colombia, though not INL employees, are a continuing reminder that we are dealing with a dangerous group of terrorists who do not respect the rules or principles of civil society.

In 2003, INL and the Colombians, working closely together, sprayed 127,000 hectares of the coca crop at 91.5 percent effectiveness, for a net of 116,000 hectares of coca eradicated. At the same time, alternative programs in Colombia resulted in the manual eradication of an additional 8,441 hectares. Similarly, we sprayed 2,821 hectares in the opium regions while 1,009 hectares were manually eradicated.

In 2002 our efforts reduced coca cultivation by 15 percent and poppy cultivation by 25 percent. With final 2003 estimates still pending, we can nevertheless see the beginning of the tong-predicted trend. Our efforts have brought us close to the tipping point where sustained suppression of illegal crops and alternative employment incentives together will convince growers that further cultivation is a futile proposition.

In Colombia, ACI funds have been vital to strengthen democracy and security.

Predictably, it is also true that the work is getting more dangerous. In 2003, INL aircraft took more than 380 hits, and we lost 4 planes. So far this year, we have taken 29 hits on our assets. We are fully reviewing our air wing operations to make the most effective use of our resources and to plan for the future. Security of our air fleet is our highest priority. We have increased intelligence coordination and protective measures to make sure each spray mission is as safe as humanly possible under the difficult circumstances. If it is not safe to launch a mission, the mission does not fly. Protecting the lives of the brave pilots who fly this program is our highest priority. Getting results of their outlay of bravery is the second, but sustaining the mission is first.

This year, as of February 29, 2004, we have sprayed over 29,000 hectares of coca and 691 hectares of poppy. This exceeds by 84 percent the amount of coca eradicated during the same timeframe in 2003. Our eradication goal for this has been initially set and is ambitious in the area of both coca and opium poppy. We have worked out a spray program in full coordination with the Colombian police and armed forces. Depending on the 2003 final spray results, we will review our spray targets for this year and adjust accordingly—because killing coca and deterring future cultivation is the twin aim. And we aim to succeed.

After 2004, we expect to enter a maintenance phase of spraying smaller, more isolated coca fields, instead of the larger fields we have sprayed since our program began. The endgame will then involve a ramp down to maintenance levels as the comprehensive effort to stabilize, eradicate coca, empower people, and restore the rule of law is achieved.

Please make no mistake: In Colombia, ACI funds have been vital to strengthen democracy and security. We have helped fund the establishment of police in 158 municipalities, many of which had not seen any government security presence in years. For the first time in history there is now a police presence in all 1098 of Colombia's municipalities. This is an enormous step forward. To demonstrate the hunger for security, San Mateo is a municipality that last had a real Colombian National Police presence in June 1999, when the FARC

[Revolutionary Armed Forces of Colombia] killed the seven San Mateo police. In April of 2003, though, our program installed a new 46-man police department, and San Mateo school children formed a human corridor and cheered as the police passed by. San Mateo declared the day a holiday, and fireworks were set off throughout the day. There is both hope and appreciation afoot—and the U.S. Congress, through leadership and support for the ACI, can take considerable credit for that development.

The results are there: In 2003, Colombia's murder rate dropped by 20 percent, [the] lowest figure since 1996. Colombia's legal armed groups committed 73 massacres in 2003, as compared to 115 in 2002. The number of victims affected by those massacres dropped 38 percent from 680 in 2002 to 418 in 2003. Also in 2003, 2,043 cases of kidnapping were registered—32 percent fewer than in 2002. Finally, 846 terrorist incidents were reported in 2003, a 49 percent drop over the 1,645 reported in 2002.

On the interdiction side we continue to work closely with Colombia's armed forces and the police. Colombian forces seized 70 metric tons of cocaine base and cocaine hydrochloride (HCl) in 2003. In addition, 126 metric tons of cannabis were seized.

The Air Bridge Denial program, which began last August [2003], is starting to become effective. Since August 2003, 10 planes suspected of drug trafficking were forced down and 8 were destroyed. In 2003, the program also resulted in 6.9 metric tons of drugs seized regionally. And as of March 1, 2004, the Colombian Air Force and its regional partners have already seized 1 metric ton of illicit drugs. But the key here is not the number of planes destroyed. Our goal is to effectively deter the use of Colombian airspace by traffickers while protecting civil aviation.

I emphasize the need to continue to work regionally. Success in Colombia can have a ripple effect for better or worse.

To be sure, the ripple effect is positive, our programs in countries bordering Colombia have also kept drug cultivation there at record low levels, increased the effectiveness and coverage of drug interdiction programs, strengthened the judiciary's ability to prosecute, and expanded economic opportunities for the poor.

ACI's administration of justice programs are designed to enhance the rule of law—to shift to a more effective criminal system, protect witnesses, increase asset seizure, and protect citizens' human rights. ACI support established 34 justice and peace houses to increase access to justice for the urban and rural poor. These *casas de justicia* (justice houses) have handled over 1.8 million cases, easing the burden on the over-taxed, inefficient judicial system. ACI funding for administration of justice also created 19 oral trial courtrooms and trained over 6,000 lawyers, judges and public defenders in new oral legal procedures designed to reduce impunity and quicken the judicial process.

Antidrug Efforts in Other Countries

In Peru and Bolivia, we have held the line on drug production so that there has not been the "balloon effect". Drug cultivation in both countries has declined 70 percent over the past five years. In Ecuador, our program along the northern border to boost security and enhance economic development has prevented any significant cultivation of drug crops in that country. Interdictions are up throughout the area. In 2003, Peru's efforts resulted in the destruction of close to 3,762 kilograms of cocaine base, 3,250 kilograms of coca paste, and 134 metric tons of coca leaf. We hope that a new drug interdiction coordination center, which we are working to establish with the Government of Peru, will assist in that effort. In Bolivia, interdiction seizures in 2003 are up to three times as high as those for 2002—with 152 metric tons of leaf and 12.9 metric tons of cocaine captured.

In Bolivia, by the end of 2003, at least 25,000 Bolivian farm families received alternative development assistance conditioned on creation of coca-free areas. As a result, the wholesale value of legitimate and legal agriculture leaving the Chapare exceeded $25 million. This represents a 25 percent increase over 2002 levels. In Peru we have also funded a key program, the "Culture of Lawfulness"—a school-based program that teaches ethics to thousands of children in junior high school. If we can mold these young people, we can help foster a civic belief that drugs and corruption are wrong. Again, this is a measure of progress. Cultural education and trust in a stable, drug-free future will take time.

In Panama, we are meanwhile funding programs to tighten port security and enhance that country's ability to investigate and prosecute financial crimes via their Financial Intelligence and Analysis units. Our increased cooperation recently reaped rich results with the expulsion of key Colombian traffickers to the United States. These are a few examples of key programs that are working in the region.

Farmers will continue to be tempted to cultivate drug crops unless they have alternative ways for feeding their families.

Antidrug Challenges

We expect our efforts in Colombia to have significant results in the next two years [2004–2006] allowing Colombia to move toward full rule of law and increasingly balanced economic development. As I noted above, we are working regionally to prevent spillover effects to neighboring countries. However, we face some serious challenges in this effort.

The first is a lack of sustained activity in terms of forced eradication programs in Bolivia and Peru. As a result, in the Yungas region of Bolivia, cultivation increased 26 percent last year to 23,550 hectares.

Despite great success in the Chapare region, where cultivation dropped 15 percent from June 2002 to June 2003, the Yungas cultivation resulted in an overall increase for the country of 17 percent to 28,450 hectares. The Yungas area poses formidable political and logistical challenges to a large eradication program, but we must, nevertheless, support efforts to tackle the problems in concert with the government of President [Carlos] Mesa.

In Peru, forced eradication programs are essentially limited to areas near labs, national parks, and new cultivation. While efforts to include a new voluntary program did help lead to a decrease in cultivation by 15 percent last year, it is very clearly forced eradication which will more quickly hurt the industry.

Growing local demand for drugs in the region is another incipient problem. These countries are painfully aware that drug consumption is on the rise, and they have launched new programs in response with U.S. support. Brazil, by some estimates, is the world's second largest consuming nation for cocaine. Brazil has initiated programs that address its growing domestic demand as well as more aggressive programs to protect its borders from use by drug traffickers. We are engaged with the government of Brazil in discussions on the major challenges it faces, and are vigorously supporting Brazil's new demand reduction emphasis.

In FY [fiscal year] 2005, our counternarcotics programs in Colombia will need to build upon the historic successes of the last few years. The relationship between drugs and terrorism in Colombia is well understood. As President [Alvaro] Uribe grapples with dismantling narco-terrorist groups, we will keep our focus on the drug industry that is funding the terrorists.

The Road Ahead

On balance, we will need to continue to work regionally in this Hemisphere, engaging with the key producing and transit countries in the ACI. So long as drugs continue to flow from the area, further efforts are needed to destroy the industry in all its forms. The traffic undermines democracy and the rule of law and, as noted, is also feeding increased demand for drugs in the region.

Given poverty rates in the region, farmers will continue to be tempted to cultivate drug crops unless they have alternative ways for feeding their families. We will therefore work collaboratively toward viable, economic options for Andean farmers and others now caught in the coercive web of the violent and illegal drug trade.

Drugs and crime undermine democracy, rule of law, and the stability required for economic development.

I am encouraged to see Andean-based efforts to regionalize counterdrug activity. With increased international cooperation and strengthening of the law enforcement agencies among our friends abroad, Congressional-supported INL programs will bring us closer to protecting our Andean neighbors, as well as enhancing our own national security. We will continue to methodically reduce the international flow of drugs and cripple the trafficking industry whose profits feed violence, violate the basic rule of law, stir hopelessness, and incite terrorism.

Our FY 2005 planning continues the pursuit of vigorous eradication and interdiction efforts to disrupt and destroy the production and transport of drugs destined for U.S. and other markets. Our request includes sustained funding for programs that will build strong government institutions capable of detecting, arresting and prosecuting processors and traffickers as well as the terrorists that thrive with them. We intend to turn over responsibilities to host nations, including counternarcotics training, equipment acquisition and operation and maintenance.

That said, I want to return to Colombia—the centerpiece of our ACI activities. We are approaching a predicted, but long-awaited tipping point. We have local, regional, hemispheric, and bipartisan U.S. leadership that finally sees the potential for—and is willing to press for—lasting change. Congress is an enormous part of this emerging picture. Our success is also a result of the vision, commitment, and energy of Colombian President Uribe. I underscore his importance to our efforts and the need for sustained support during the remaining years of his presidency. We are here because of all those who helped conceive and push forward U.S. support to ACI—and also because of our strong partnership with President Uribe, whose policy goals are in exact alignment with our own.

Drugs and crime undermine democracy, rule of law, and the stability required for economic development. The drug trade continues to kill our young people, and the bulk of the drugs arriving in the United States still come from the Andean region. The drug trade also funds terrorists in this Hemisphere and other regions. These are the stark realities.

Set against them is our methodical ACI program, in its many parts. And that program is producing results. Projects in Colombia, Bolivia, Peru Ecuador, Brazil, Venezuela, and Panama are integrated. I am making sure that our assets are being used in the most effective manner and that performance criteria for projects are strengthened in order to better measure results. We have reached a tipping point in Colombia— for the first time we may be close to delivering a lasting blow to narco-terrorists. Sustained support for President Uribe is essential. . . . In all of this, there is a real mission. And in the mission, there is the real potential for lasting results that will change our world—for the better.

The United States Must Win the War on Drugs

Lou Dobbs

Lou Dobbs is a television and radio news anchor, columnist, and author.

We're fighting a war that is inflicting even greater casualties than the wars in Iraq and Afghanistan and, incredibly, costing even more money. We're losing the War on Drugs, and we've been in retreat for three decades.

Losing the War on Drugs

That statement may come as a surprise to John Walters, Director of the White House Office of National Drug Control Policy, who spent last week [February 4–10, 2007] trumpeting the [President George W.] Bush administration's anti-drug policies. He claims these policies have led to a decline in drug abuse and improvements in our physical and mental health.

While Walters focused on a marginal decline in drug use, he made no mention of the shocking rise in drug overdoses. The Centers for Disease Control and Prevention this week reported unintentional drug overdoses nearly doubled over the course of five years, rising from 11,155 in 1999 to 19,838 in 2004. Fatal drug overdoses in teenagers and young adults soared 113 percent.

More than 22 million Americans were classified with substance abuse or dependence problems in 2005, according to the Substance Abuse and Mental Health Services Administration. Nearly 8,000 people are trying drugs for the first time every day—that's about 3 million a year. The majority of new users are younger than 18, and more than half of them are female.

Lou Dobbs, "The War Within, Killing Ourselves," *CNN.com*, February 14, 2007. © Cable News Network. Reproduced by permission.

Obviously, John Walters and I are not looking at the same statistics. There is simply no excuse for permitting the destruction of so many young lives.

How can anyone rationalize the fact that the United States, with only 4 percent of the world's population, consumes two-thirds of the world's illegal drugs?

Former President Richard Nixon first declared a modern-day war on the use of illicit substances, calling drugs "public enemy number one" and pushing through the Controlled Substances Act of 1970. Since then the government has waged a futile, three-decades-long war of attrition.

Illicit drug use costs the United States almost $200 billion a year, according to the National Institute on Drug Abuse [NIDA] include alcohol and tobacco-related costs along with health care, criminal justice and lost productivity and the figure exceeds $500 billion annually.

We must commit ourselves as members of this great society to only one option in the War on Drugs—victory.

Treatment for Drug Addiction

Even with new rehabilitation centers and clinics, less than 20 percent of drug and alcohol abusers receive the treatment they need and the cycle of drug-related crime continues unabated.

It's estimated about half of the more than two million inmates in our nation's prisons meet the clinical criteria for drug or alcohol dependence, and yet fewer than one-fifth of these offenders receive any kind of treatment. Studies show successful treatment cuts drug abuse in half, reduces criminal activity by as much 80 percent and reduces arrests by up to 64 percent.

As NIDA reports, "Treatment not only lowers recidivism rates, it is also cost-effective. It is estimated that for every dollar spent on addiction treatment programs, there is a $4 to $7 reduction in the cost of drug-related crimes. With some out-patient programs, total savings can exceed costs by a ratio of 12:1."

In the midst of the global war on terror along with wars in Iraq and Afghanistan, we have forgotten about the brutal effects of narcotics trafficking on millions of American lives. We must end the abuse of drugs and alcohol, and provide successful treatment for Americans whose addictions are destroying their own lives and wounding our families and society.

Whatever course we follow in prosecuting other wars, we must commit ourselves as members of this great society to only one option in the War on Drugs—victory.

The War on Drugs Cannot Be Won by Fighting Drug Trafficking

Gary Becker

Gary Becker is a professor of economics and sociology at the University of Chicago.

Every American president since [Richard] Nixon has engaged in a "war" on illegal drugs: cocaine, heroin, hashish, and the like. And every president without exception has lost this war. The explanation lies not in a lack of effort—indeed, I believe there has been too much effort—but rather in a basic property of the demand for drugs, and the effects of trying to reduce consumption of a good like drugs by punishing persons involved in its trade.

> The war on drugs is costing the U.S. one way or another well over $100 billion per year.

The war on drugs is fought by trying to apprehend producers and distributors of drugs, and then to punish them rather severely if convicted. The expected punishment raises the price that suppliers of drugs need to receive in order for them to be willing to take the considerable risks involved in the drug trade. The higher price discourages purchase and consumption of illegal drugs, as with legal goods and services. The harder the war is fought, the greater the expected punishment, the higher is the street price of drugs, and generally the smaller is the consumption of drugs.

Those suppliers who are caught and punished do not do very well, which is the typical result for the many small fry in

Gary Becker, "The Failure of the War on Drugs," *Becker-Posner Blog*, March 20, 2005. Reproduced by permission of the author.

volved in distributing drugs. On the other hand, those who manage to avoid punishment—sometimes through bribes and other corrupting behavior—often make large profits because the price is raised so high.

An Inefficient Drug Policy

This approach can be effective if say every 10% increase in drug prices has a large negative effect on the use of drugs. This is called an elastic demand. However, the evidence from more than a dozen studies strongly indicates that the demand for drugs is generally quite inelastic; that is, a 10% rise in their prices reduces demand only by about 5%, which means an elasticity of about 1/2. This implies that as drug prices rise, real spending on drugs increases, in this case, by about 5% for every 10% increase in price. So if the war on drugs increased the price of drugs by at least 200%—estimates suggest this increase is about right—spending on drugs would have increased enormously, which it did.

This increased spending is related to increased real costs of suppliers in the form of avoidance of detection, bribery payments, murder of competitors and drug agents, primitive and dangerous production methods, and the like. In addition, the country pays directly in the form of the many police shifted toward fighting drugs, court time and effort spent on drug offenders, and the cost of imprisonment. The US spends about $40,000 per year per prisoner, and in recent years a sizeable fraction of both federal and state prisoners have been convicted on drug-related charges.

After totaling all spending, a study by Kevin Murphy, Steve Cicala, and myself estimates that the war on drugs is costing the US one way or another well over $100 billion per year. These estimates do not include important intangible costs, such as the destructive effects on many inner city neighborhoods, the use of the American military to fight drug lords and farmers in Colombia and other nations, or the corrupting influence of drugs on many governments.

A Better Way

Assuming an interest in reducing drug consumption—will pay little attention here to whether that is a good goal—is there a better way to do that than by these unsuccessful wars? Our study suggests that legalization of drugs combined with an excise tax on consumption would be a far cheaper and more effective way to reduce drug use. Instead of a war, one could have, for example, a 200% tax on the legal use of drugs by all adults—consumption by say persons under age 18 would still be illegal. That would reduce consumption in the same way as the present war, and would also increase total spending on drugs, as in the current system.

> *Legalization of drugs combined with an excise tax on consumption would be a far cheaper and more effective way to reduce drug use.*

But the similarities end at that point. The tax revenue from drugs would accrue to state and federal authorities, rather than being dissipated into the real cost involving police, imprisonment, dangerous qualities, and the like. Instead of drug cartels, there would be legal companies involved in production and distribution of drugs of reliable quality, as happened after the prohibition of alcohol ended. There would be no destruction of poor neighborhoods—so no material for *The Wire* HBO series, or the movie *Traffic*—no corruption of Afghani or Columbian governments, and no large scale imprisonment of African-American and other drug suppliers. The tax revenue to various governments hopefully would substitute for other taxes, or would be used for educating young people about any dangersous effects of drugs.

To be sure, there would be some effort by suppliers of drugs to avoid taxes by going underground with their production and distribution. But since there would then be a option to produce legally—there is no such option now—the movement underground would be much less than under the present system. As a result, the police could concentrate its efforts more effectively on a greatly reduced underground drug sector. We have seen how huge taxes on cigarettes in New York and elsewhere have been implemented without massive movement of production and distribution underground in order to avoid the taxes.

So legalization could have a greater effect in reducing drug use than a war on drugs without all the large and disturbing system costs. How high the tax rate should be would be determined by social policy. This approach could accommodate a libertarian policy with legalization and low excise taxes, a socially "conservative" position that wants to greatly reduce drug use with very high tax rates, and most positions in between these two extremes. So if drug consumption was not considered so bad once it became legal, perhaps the tax would be small, as with alcoholic beverages in the US. Or perhaps the pressure would be great for very high taxes, as with cigarettes. But whatever the approach, it could be implemented far more successfully by legalizing drugs than by further efforts to heat up the failing war on illegal drugs.

Global Drug Trafficking Cannot Be Stopped

Moisés Naím

Moisés Naím is the editor in chief of Foreign Policy *magazine; previously, he was the Venezuelan minister of trade and industry and an executive director at the World Bank. He is also the author of* Illicit: How Smugglers, Traffickers, and Copycats Are Hijacking the Global Economy, *from which the following selection is excerpted.*

Every business has its stock characters, the drug business perhaps more than most: the dealer, the courier, the drug lord, the kingpin, as we are used to seeing them in the movies. The man I met one afternoon in an elegant restaurant in a Mexican border town fit none of these descriptions. Yet people like him play a crucial role in the drug trade today. They are hard to identify because they hide in plain sight. They are hard to take out, because their involvement in the trade is just one aspect of their business, lost in the stream of legitimate commerce. They are traffickers nearly by accident—the accident, that is, of running into a line of business too juicy to refuse.

Don Alfonzo (not his real name) is an exuberant man in his sixties and a proud father. He began our lunchtime conversation by telling me that his two children had graduated—with honors, he specified—from top U.S. universities and were now pursuing successful careers in art and medicine in Mexico City. He explained that his family had long owned a medium-size construction company. It was in the mid-1990s that Don Alfonzo found himself—almost inadvertently, but not quite—venturing into the "transportation" business.

Transporting Drugs

He first learned about the details and mechanics of drug smuggling when he decided to find out the real cause of the high turnover rate among his company's truck drivers. He discovered that with just one border crossing carrying a relatively small shipment of drugs, his drivers made the equivalent of one year's salary. Naturally, after making such a killing their truck-driving job was no longer appealing or needed. Through his inquiry, Alfonzo also found out that the funders who put up the money for the drivers to purchase the drugs were upstart members of the local business community and well-known politicians, who made a huge profit on their loans. The loans bore little risk because the drivers were rarely caught. Besides, in the prevailing honor code repayment was very important. "Finally," Don Alfonzo said, "one day, and almost out of boredom and curiosity, I told one of my trusted employees who I knew was using our trucks for smuggling that it was only fair that he share some of the profits with the company. He immediately accepted and, as they say, the rest is history."

He continued: "Since then, I got involved more frequently, mostly as a financier, and while we did it only about once a month the profits were several times larger than what we made in construction. Although we continued with our construction business, I must tell you that sometimes I think that in this town the construction business is riskier than moving drugs across."

I asked Don Alfonzo if he was not concerned with the personal risks he was running. He smiled. "What do you mean?" he said. "I am just a small businessman who lends money to his employees, and what they do with that is their own business. You know, there are thousands like me. The gringos and the police here are busy chasing the big guys, and if they go after the small guys like us they will need to build a new jail the size of this whole town. The economy of this entire region would go bankrupt. No government can touch this. Why should they? The big guys give good theater and are good for politics. We don't."

Not too long after this conversation, Mexico's long-running drug wars went through another of their periodic, spectacular flare-ups. This time it turned out that the leaders of two drug organizations that had been longtime rivals, the Arellano Felix organization and the Gulf Cartel, had forged an alliance in the high-security prison in which they were being held after having been arrested in much-celebrated raids by the *federales* [federal police]. From their prison lodgings the new allies were running a vicious campaign against an aggressive new player, Joaquin "El Chapo" Guzmán, an outlaw said to be sheltered by the population in his home state of Sinaloa. The warden of the prison had been bought off. As for the seriousness of the threat posed by Guzmán, it became abundantly clear when a member of President Vicente Fox's travel advance team was arrested on suspicion of ties to him.

No one believes that poppy growing will stop being Afghanistan's main economic activity any time soon.

Patterns of the past suggest that Guzmán will eventually be arrested or killed, by *federales* or by other criminals. That victory too will be transient. For Don Alfonzo and the many other respectable citizens, businessmen, and officials of his ilk who help sustain the drug trade, business will keep on chugging and money will keep getting made. It's one of the seeming contradictions of the drug business that on further inspection are not contradictions at all. That one high-profile criminal rises to replace another is a fairly easy notion to absorb. But today they are the tip of the iceberg. The diffusion of the drug business into the fiber of local and global economic life is much harder to fathom, let alone combat. Its political implications are ominous. Yet, more than any cartel, kingpin, or rebel warlord, it is this pervasive global main-streaming of the business that the fight against drugs is up against today.

The U.S. Drug Market

Other, perhaps more familiar paradoxes of the drug trade only confirm this realization. Consider Washington, D.C. It is the hub of the war on drugs, the most massive, expensive, and technologically advanced antidrug offensive in history. In and around the capital, thousands of federal employees report daily to jobs that exist solely to combat the drug trade and enforce drug laws. Some are Drug Enforcement Administration (DEA) agents, or staff in the White House drug policy office, home to the so-called drug czar. Others are drug specialists in dozens of other agencies and services, from Immigration and Customs Enforcement (ICE) to the U.S. Marshals, Secret Service, FBI [Federal Bureau of Investigation], Coast Guard, and more. They are cogs in a vast machinery that consumes around $20 billion per year at the federal level alone in the fight against drug use and trade. Nationally, the fight brings in 1.7 million arrests and 250,000 incarcerations each year. In Washington, 28 percent of inmates are incarcerated primarily for drug charges.

Yet minutes away from these offices are Washington's sixty open-air drug markets that serve suburbanites cruising for a fix, local retailers and intermediaries who take the product to upscale neighborhoods. And the market is thriving. Supply is abundant and prices are steady, hallmarks of a volume business. The purity levels of heroin are rising. There are products for every taste and budget, from high-end sniffables for the rich kids and bankers to vials of crack cocaine and cheap heroin blends suitable only for injection and destined for the hard addicts. (The cheap stuff can always be found in the vicinity of methadone clinics.) With this market offering something for everyone, it's little surprise that nearly one Washingtonian in two above the age of twelve admits to having used an illicit drug. Meanwhile only fifty kilograms of cocaine and thirty-four kilograms of heroin were seized in the District in 2004. The numbers are trivial compared with the visible trade taking place each day on the streets. And it's consolation only to the most jaded Washingtonians that down the road in Baltimore, the situation is even worse.

In Washington, a city famously divided by income and race, the drug economy connects segments of local society more effectively than any almost anything else. . . .

At the command center of the war on drugs, a stronger force is winning: the market.

In Colombia new strains of the coca plant that are resistant to herbicides have emerged.

The Global Drug Market

This is the case not just at the command center but on the front lines as well. In Afghanistan, for example, the opium poppies are back with a vengeance. In 1999, Afghanistan produced more than five thousand tons of opium, smashing its own record. The next year, the Taliban outlawed the crop, having deemed it un-Islamic. Cynics argued that the Taliban's aim was to cause a price rise and benefit by selling stockpiles at a massive profit. At any rate, production plummeted to a mere two hundred tons in 2001, all of it in the far north of the country, beyond Taliban reach. By the end of that year, the United States and its allies had driven the Islamic militia out of power, and the new government in Kabul, led by Hamid Karzai, immediately renewed the opium ban. But the poppies swept back, reclaiming prime land in all parts of the country, overrunning fields once devoted to wheat. Within a year, opium poppy acreage nearly matched its 1999 level. By 2004, Afghanistan was producing an estimated 4,200 tons of opium from 323,700 hectares. The Karzai government also launched an intensive effort to dissuade growers from planting the poppies. But no one believes that poppy growing will stop being Afghanistan's main economic activity any time soon.

The opportunity is just too rich. Even though the Afghan grower earns only a microscopic fraction of what his plants will generate down the line—after the opium has been refined into morphine, then heroin, then cut with substances like quinine or baking powder and distributed into U.S. or European streets—it is still far and away the land's most lucrative use. It is convenient, too: poppies require less water than wheat does, and the sap does not rot. Besides, Afghans are managing now to capture a bit more of the margin. In the past, opium was shipped raw; now, laboratories that refine it into higher-value narcotics are springing up all over the country. One impact of the business is to drive up the price of labor. A *Washington Post* reporter found that in one northern village, it recently cost ten dollars to buy a day of work that previously fetched only three dollars. The local police earn thirty dollars per month, assuming they're paid at all. A hundred-dollar cash bribe buys a lot of goodwill.

The news from another well-known front is not much better. In Colombia, fifteen years and billions of dollars in U.S. spending to support the Colombian military in counternarcotics efforts have netted some successes: the decapitation of the Medellin and Cali cartels and scores of arrests, extraditions, and convictions resulting in long sentences in U.S. jails. Yet the drugs still flow. The left-wing FARC [Revolutionary Armed Forces of Colombia] guerrillas and their right-wing opponents, the AUC [United Self-Defense Forces of Colombia] "self-defense" forces, both control coca-growing territory, shelter cocaine labs, and collect revenues on drug exports that make up 50 percent of FARC's and up to 70 percent of the AUC's cash flow. Trafficking interests reach high into the political and military establishment. Colombia not only produces most of the world's cocaine but has now become a serious player in heroin as well, thanks to the widespread planting of poppies from Asia in the 1990s. As for the massive crop-fumigation programs that the United States has bank-rolled, the drug networks have an answer, too: research and development. Diminished acreage no longer means lower production, as the traffickers are applying the latest agronomy techniques to boost their productivity. In Colombia new strains of the coca plant that are resistant to herbicides have emerged. They also happen to be leafier, grow up to twice the height of the traditional plant, and result in much purer and stronger cocaine.

It takes only one kilogram of cocaine to command $12,000 to $35,000.

Technology has also allowed new entrants to participate in this lucrative market. The most coveted (and therefore expensive), marijuana is no longer cultivated in the tropical jungles of Colombia or Mexico. It comes from British Columbia in Canada. The variety known as "B.C. bud" is grown using advanced hydroponics and cloning techniques in special nurseries that keep the temperature and other conditions at optimal levels throughout the year. As Sarah Kershaw of the *New York Times* reported, a rugged, hard-to-patrol border poses more problems for the police than it does for the kayakers who navigate the rapids with loads of up to one hundred pounds of B.C. bud, which sells for $3,500 a pound in California, and who coordinate deliveries by means of BlackBerry two-way devices. The B.C. bud business also involves moving cocaine and weapons back from the United States to Canada. According to Canadian law enforcement officials, this industry has grown to a gigantic $7 billion-a-year business in 2005. A decade ago it barely existed.

The End of Illusions

Despite the global nature of the trade, public attention is still focused on the usual fronts: the United States for demand, Colombia, Mexico, Afghanistan, and a few others for supply. It's not completely unjustified. Far and away the United States remains the single largest consumer country for illegal drugs. It is also the motor of the global response, often deploying its political or military might beyond its borders in service of its approach to drug control. At the other end of the supply chain, it is also true that Colombia and Afghanistan are the largest single sources of cocaine and heroin, respectively. These are stubborn facts that predate the 1990s.

But taken in isolation these facts imply a map of the world that is highly misleading. For during the 1990s, the number of countries reporting serious drug addiction problems steadily rose. Spikes in HIV/AIDS infections became a macabre re-vealer of new trade routes for injectable drugs. Amid steady growth of the world drug market, the big three—marijuana, cocaine, and opiates—lost market share to methamphetamine, rougher and more potent and addictive than heroin. The meth epidemic joins in a common crisis the small towns in the U.S. heartland and virtually every social category in Thailand, where methamphetamine is known as "yaa baa" (crazy drug) and used as a stimulant for work as well as pleasure. Other compounds—Ecstasy, ketamine, GHB, and Rohypnol—are on the rise as well. Because these drugs are chemicals that do not depend on plant inputs, they can be manufactured virtually anywhere that some basic supplies can be obtained and a makeshift lab established. But this doesn't mean that they are restricted to a cottage industry. The meth that kills an over-dosing teenager in Missouri is as likely to have come in a bulk shipment from Canada or Mexico as to have been concocted locally in someone's garage.

The global explosion of demand and supply has shattered the illusion of invulnerability that governments—or, for that matter, public opinion—harbored in many countries. Now, no country is isolated enough to delude itself or its critics into imagining that it has no part in the world drug trade. Countries that long harbored the illusion that they were only "transshipment" locations have woken up to the fact that they have become themselves major suppliers, consumers, or both. . . .

Launder, Barter, Hack

This global industry transformation would not have been possible without the innovations and tools of globalization. During the 1990s the number of reported drug seizures worldwide, which had been stagnant at around 300,000 per year, more than quadrupled to 1.4 million in 2001. This explosion should come as no surprise, for the entire legal and technological apparatus of globalization has made the illicit drug trade faster, more efficient, and easier to hide. It all starts with volume: with daily traffic of about 550 cargo containers only at the port of Hong Kong or 63 million passengers a year at London's Heathrow Airport (1,250 flights per day), the compact nature of illicit drugs makes them the equivalent of the needle in the haystack. A million-dollar retail payload of high-grade marijuana, say a thousand pounds, fits handily in a false compartment of one of the 4.5 million trucks crossing the U.S.-Mexican border every year. It takes only one kilogram of cocaine to command $12,000 to $35,000. Heroin is still more weight-efficient. A single mule who smuggles powder drugs by air or on foot, ingesting them wrapped in honey-coated condoms, can carry, fully laden, enough South American high-grade heroin to command $50,000 to $200,000.

> *Many large-scale exchanges in the global underworld . . . involve drugs as collateral or compensation.*

Everywhere, the methods of the trade reflect the advance and spread of new technologies. Not only can drug wholesalers use express delivery services, but by tracking a shipment online they can know whether it has arrived or whether it has been held up, alerting them to a possible interception and narrowing the window in which authorities can intervene before the traffickers take evasive action. Drug sales are routinely arranged on cell phones that are discarded after no more than a week's use; traffickers coordinate by means of Instant Messaging, Webmail accounts, and chatrooms, often at public and anonymous computers in cybercafes. More sophisticated networks employ their own specialized hackers to protect their communications and "hack back" into law enforcement machines trying to penetrate them. The same security standards, like encryption, that make it safe to buy a book from Amazon.com or contribute to a political campaign online also help drug traffickers conceal their communications, transactions, and identities. Small-timers benefit too: the Internet brims with mail-order sales of marijuana seeds, equipment with which to grow high-potency hydroponic weed in a closet in one's home, and instructions for home-cooking methamphetamine and other substances.

It is perhaps the financial revolution of the past ten years that has most benefited the drug trade. If a packet of heroin is a needle in the haystack of world trade volumes, its monetary value is even harder to pick out in the daily swirl of financial transactions. To conceal the movement of money, pay suppliers, remunerate operatives, and recirculate the proceeds, drug traffickers make use of the complete gamut—from cash stuffed in the mail or carried in small amounts by couriers known as "smurfs" to complex laundering operations involving front companies, offshore banks, and correspondents and intermediaries in multiple countries. E-commerce, Internet banking, and wire transfer services all come into play.

In some cases, the drug-money circulation system is so entrenched and institutionalized that it develops its own "brand". In the scheme known as the Black Market Peso Exchange

(BMPE), Colombian drug traffickers repatriate their proceeds by entrusting the dollars to brokers, who use the funds to make purchases in the United States on behalf of Colombian customers at a favorable exchange rate. The customers pay the brokers in pesos that the brokers pass on to the traffickers—after collecting their fee, of course. The system highlights the growing role of intermediaries and the intertwining of "dirty" and "clean" money. It also shows how law-abiding manufacturers in the United States can end up being paid, albeit indirectly, with drug money. The BMPE has worked so well that it has spawned numerous variants. It now encompasses Mexico as well, offering more opportunities for intermediaries to take shelter behind multiple frontiers. It recycles an estimated $5 billion annually.

Alongside these modern methods, more ancient ones still have their use, such as barter. Drugs make good currency in exotic settings. In-kind payments are common in many distribution networks; much of the product that seeps out along the trade routes is used as a means of payment and in the process often creates large populations of addicts in countries where only ten years ago there were none. But many large-scale exchanges in the global underworld also involve drugs as collateral or compensation. In the late 1990s, the Russian mafia supplied Mexican drug traffickers with automatic weapons, radars, and even miniature submarines in exchange for cocaine, amphetamines, and heroin. The IRA [Irish Republican Army] is reputed to supply the Dublin heroin market, and IRA officers surfaced in Colombia in 2001, providing technical advice and training in weapons and tactics and of course European drug market outlets to the FARC. And in remote locations where currency is scarce or impractical, heroin or cocaine make fine substitutes, easy to carry and universally valued—a modern-day salt, the prized white powder for our times.

The United States Cannot Stop Drugs from Being Grown in Latin America

Ted Galen Carpenter

Ted Galen Carpenter is the vice president for defense and foreign policy studies at the Cato Institute. He is also the author of Bad Neighbor Policy: Washington's Futile War on Drugs in Latin America, *from which the following selection is excerpted.*

Frustration with the limited effects of interdiction efforts is one factor that has led U.S. and Latin American officials to place more emphasis on crop eradication. [Kevin Jack] Riley [an analyst at the RAND Corporation] notes the working of that logic with respect to the cocaine trade: "Coca is the essential ingredient in cocaine, and without it the traffickers would be driven out of business. Coca plants themselves represent the most visible—and, thus, vulnerable—point in the production chain. Certainly coca fields are much easier to detect than small bundles of cocaine."

Eradication Programs

The United States has supported both forced eradication of drug crops and compensated eradication programs. Both versions have encountered serious problems. Forced eradication risks alienating sizable portions of the population in drug-source countries. Vehement resistance to forced eradication by the peasantry in Bolivia was a major reason why successive governments resisted U.S. pressure during the 1980s. Peru under the government of Alberto Fujimori exhibited similar reluctance. The forced eradication component of Plan Colombia certainly is arousing a great deal of public opposition and confirms that the reluctance of the Bolivian and Peruvian governments was well founded.

But compensated eradication has its own difficulties. Among other problems, it can become a vehicle for milking the United States of aid money. In Bolivia, for example, the United States established a compensation level of $2,000 for every hectare (2.471 acres) of coca taken out of cultivation. That level was set in November 1986. By the early 1990s, coca growers were pressing for an increase to $6,000 per hectare, to reflect the higher potential value of coca on the illegal market. U.S. officials strongly opposed increasing the compensation level, arguing that $6,000 per hectare would act as an incentive to plant new coca and cash it in.

Both U.S. and Latin American officials never seem to lose their touching faith in the efficacy of crop eradication programs. In January 1976 the official in charge of Operation Condor in Mexico predicted confidently that, with the use of herbicides, "before mid-year we are going to completely end the cultivation of drugs in this country." A quarter century later, the claims made for the eradication efforts in Peru, Bolivia, and Colombia are only a shade less audacious.

The attitude of U.S. officials about the progress of the international phase of the drug war has a dreary consistency. Setbacks are ignored or explained away; every sign of success is touted, often to the point of absurdity; and victory is said to be just around the corner—if the current policies continue awhile longer. The proclamations of prospective breakthroughs occur so frequently that one is reminded of the person who asserts that it is easy to quit smoking: after all, he has done so numerous times. . . .

Drug policy analysts Patrick L. Clawson and Rensselaer W. Lee III describe the many unintended consequences associated with drug-eradication programs. They note that eradication in existing production areas may simply drive farmers into more remote areas, "thereby opening up new production areas—a pattern that has been repeated numerous times in both Bolivia and Peru." Eradication also may encourage farmers to make every effort to increase yields on the remaining acreage. Between 1990 and 1995, for example, the area cultivated in coca in Bolivia fell 3 percent while the amount of leaf harvested rose 10 percent. Clawson and Lee also note that eradication can be a de facto coca price support program. After all, the whole point of eradication is to reduce the supply of coca. Basic economic laws of supply and demand suggest that prices for the remaining crops would then tend to rise. Clawson and Lee point out that the voluntary acreage reduction programs so popular with both U.S. officials and leaders in the Andean countries "are similar to the crop acreage reduction programs that the U.S. government uses to raise the income of wheat farmers. It is not clear why Washington thinks that a crop reduction program raises the income of Midwest wheat farmers but lowers the income of Andean coca farmers." Riley echoes their point: "Compensation establishes a floor price. When coca prices are above the compensation price, farmers have no economic incentive to eradicate. When prices are below the floor, the compensation provides the farmers an income and thus helps underwrite the downside risk associated with coca farming. In other words, the only way a farmer will not benefit is if he grows no coca at all."

Farmers can make 4, and sometimes 10, times the income growing coca than they can raising legal crops.

The Crop Substitution Mirage

As evidence mounts that eradication and interdiction efforts produce minimal results and that "victory" in the drug war is as elusive as ever, policymakers invariably start to place greater emphasis on crop substitution and economic development programs. We have gone through that cycle several times during the past three decades.

Even to many critics of the drug war, crop substitution appears to be a less draconian way to seek to reduce the supply of illegal drugs. Its rationale is to give Latin American *campesinos* [farmers], viable economic alternatives to participation in the illicit cocaine, marijuana, or opium trade. But the record of crop substitution programs should dissuade U.S. officials from continuing to pursue that panacea. Neither the narrow version (providing financial subsidies to induce farmers to switch to legal crops) nor the broader concept (providing infrastructure assistance to make legal agricultural—and nonagricultural—enterprises economically viable) has achieved worthwhile results.

Over the years, U.S. officials have repeatedly worked with their Latin American counterparts to induce growers to abandon the cultivation of drug crops for legal alternatives. They have suggested a prolific array of substitutes, including bananas, maize, rice, coffee, citrus fruit, and various grains. Economic realities usually doom such efforts. For example, farmers can make 4, and sometimes more than 10, times the income growing coca than they can raising legal crops. Drug policy scholar LaMond Tullis provides an even higher estimate of the advantage. He contends that, in many areas "illegal-drug growers can make from ten to fifty times more in provisioning the illegal drug market than they can in any other agricultural pursuit." Although the income advantage varies greatly from country to country (and region to region within a country) as well as on the type of drug crop in question, the advantage is usually quite substantial. It is not comforting when two leading analysts conclude that in Colombia, UN [United Nations] "data on net income from various crops show that the only crop anywhere near coca is opium poppy."

Advantages of Drug Crops

Drug crops have other important advantages. Coca and marijuana (and even opium poppies) can be grown in remote regions with poor soil—places in which alternate crops are not economically feasible. Clawson and Lee note that the advantage is especially evident with regard to coca: "Coca is a hardy and adaptable perennial shrub. . . . It flourishes on steep slopes and in infertile acidic soils, that is, in conditions that restrict the growth of other crops. Coca can grow almost anywhere in tropical South America and in tropical regions of the world generally." That fact alone underscores the inherent difficulty confronting both eradication and crop substitution initiatives.

Drug crops also can yield faster returns. Coca bushes can be harvested a mere 18 months after planting and can provide maximum yields in three years or so. A well-tended bush can also produce for as many as 25 years. Many alternative cash crops require four or more years from planting to first harvest. Coca provides up to six harvests a year whereas most other crops come into season just once a year.

In addition, coca tends to be easier to market. Harvested leaves spoil relatively slowly, and they do not damage easily during transport. Moreover, as one farmer in Peru's Upper Huallaga Valley bluntly told international officials: "Buyers go to the farms to get the coca. If I plant any other crop I must get it to market and spend money transporting it. That does not happen with coca." The importance of the cash-and-carry policies of coca buyers in countries with inadequate transportation systems should not be underestimated. The trip from the Upper Huallaga Valley to Lima, for example, is a grinding 35-hour journey, primarily in second gear.

Because they operate outside the law, drug-crop growers do not have to deal with many of the obstacles that farmers of legal crops must endure. Those obstacles include poor transportation infrastructure, lack of access to credit, lack of reasonable and consistent government standards for recognizing titles to property (as well as a lack of efficient enforcement of property rights), and volatile, unpredictable markets for agricultural products. Buyers for trafficking organizations merely purchase the crops, pay the growers well, and haul off the crops. Not surprisingly, a significant percentage of Latin American farmers prefer to do business that way even if it means dealing in an illegal product.

Other Crop Substitution Problems

Although they express some optimism for the potential of crop substitution programs, Clawson and Lee concede: "Many barriers stand in the way of switching from coca to legal crops, such as fragile ecologies with dubious potential for legal cultivation, isolation from major markets, severe political and law and order problems, and the ease of growing and selling coca." A United States Agency for International Development (USAID) study was even more pessimistic: "The crop substitution strategy . . . has been unsuccessful in introducing substitute crops and in controlling illicit cultivation, at least in the limited span of a typical development initiative. Viable substitute crops are difficult to identify given the generally unfavorable climatic conditions and poorly developed infrastructures that characterize most remote poppy- and coca-growing areas. In many instances, there are not alternative crops that can be grown profitably." Even when there are crops that theoretically can compete with coca and other drug crops, there are usually problems that undermine their competitive advantage. Brookings Institution scholar Paul B. Stares notes one typical problem: "Some crop substitution programs have reported higher overall returns from certain licit crops. Studies have also identified other agricultural products that have the promise to be just as profitable, if not more so. The basic problem, however, is that these more lucrative crops are typically consumed locally, and local markets are not large enough to sustain a large-scale shift in production."

Sometimes well-meaning initiatives by U.S. aid workers lead to disastrous results for Latin American farmers. A few years ago officials for USAID convinced peasants in the Upper

Huallaga Valley that growing achiote (a local food crop) would be more profitable than growing coca. The farmers proceeded to plant achiote in large quantities. When it came time to sell, however, the price had plummeted and, thanks to USAID prodding, there was so much overproduction that some of the achiote could not be sold at all. Needless to say, the farmers were not thrilled at the results of that crop substitution program.

Similar developments occurred in Bolivia. U.S. experts talked one group of farmers into planting ginger. After accumulating 40 tons of the plant, they were urged to halt production because there was no market for that much ginger. The coca farmers who had switched to bananas, grapefruit, and pineapples fared no better. James Painter, BBC correspondent for Latin America, describes the crop substitution fiasco in the Chapare engineered by Washington and La Paz in the early 1990s: "The Chapare is full of rotting oranges, lemons, and grapefruit. Oversupply, high transportation costs, and long distances to markets mean that often it is simply not worth a farmer's even picking them off the ground where they fall."

Crop substitution programs, like eradication and interdiction efforts, ignore some of the most basic principles of economics.

Even when some coca, marijuana, and poppy growers are willing to take their fields out of production in exchange for U.S. financial largess, there is little to stop other entrepreneurs from entering the market. Indeed, even current producers often simply pocket the money and resume operations in another location. There are indications that Bolivian, Peruvian, and Colombian participants in crop substitution programs have done exactly that. Ironically, aid from the United States or the indigenous government may provide growers with additional capital to expand their production.

Alternative Development

The mounting evidence of the failure of crop substitution programs has impelled U.S. officials to emphasize broader alternative economic development programs to induce farmers and laborers involved in the drug trade to pursue other options. Such programs have fared little better than crop substitution efforts. In fact, economic development projects can simply provide additional capital and other benefits to those who have no intention of abandoning the drug trade. For example, aid monies to improve the transportation infrastructure in recipient countries by building modern roads into remote areas make it easier for drug farmers to get their crops to market and may open new areas to drug cultivation. That situation became so evident in Bolivia's Chapare region during the late 1980s and early 1990s that USAID stopped funding road construction projects. The Drug Enforcement Administration (DEA) took even more drastic action, actually blowing up existing roadways in the Chapare.

Building manufacturing facilities in such regions (even in those rare cases in which the projects are economically justified) also tends to have a supplemental rather than a substitutional effect. In other words, drug-crop farmers do not give up their traditional livelihood and replace it with their new jobs; they merely add the income from that new job to the existing illegal source of income.

The bottom line is that the black market premium in the illegal drug trade creates an irresistible temptation for a substantial portion of the agricultural sector in drug-producing countries. Drug-trafficking organizations can outbid the competition from buyers of legal crops, and usually can do so quite easily. The notion that the potential income from bananas, maize, or citrus fruit can compete with the potential income from coca, marijuana, or opium poppies is about as realistic as assuming that a burger flipper at McDonald's can earn as much as a software designer for Microsoft.

True, some farmers will refuse to be drawn into the drug trade because of its illegality. Some may object to drug trafficking on moral grounds; others may simply want to avoid it out of fear of criminal penalties or other government retaliation. But many will swallow any moral qualms they might have, and even incur the risk of criminal sanctions, given the sizable profit potential. And the drug-trafficking organizations can bid up the price to whatever level is necessary to ensure an adequate supply of the product. Crop substitution programs, like eradication and interdiction efforts, ignore some of the most basic principles of economics. That is why they are inevitably doomed to fail.

A Failed Policy

Both U.S. and Latin American leader have been impervious to that reality. Crop substitution schemes have been tried and found wanting for more than a quarter of a century—extraordinarily long record of failure. To be blunt, crop substitution strategies have worked no better than other exercises in central economic planning around the world. One would think even the most determined officials would finally learn that lesson.

Unfortunately, that does not seem to be the case. Shortly after his election as president of Peru in June 2001, Alejandro Toledo emphasized crop substitution as a solution to the plague of commerce in illegal drugs. He stated that alternative crops—coffee, cocoa, cotton, rice, bananas, and papaya—were the way forward in the battle against coca leaf production. Indeed, he added a wrinkle to the usual crop substitution strategy. Toledo stressed, "I believe in crop substitution that generates work. That means pulling up coca leaf. People will be paid to pull it up. And then, in a second phase, come other crops." In other words, he wanted to create a make-work, public works program out of crop substitution. He apparently was unfamiliar with the concept of opportunity cost as well if he believed that pulling up coca plants was the most efficient use of time for Peruvian workers.

Yet even Toledo implicitly acknowledges that alternative crops cannot compete economically with coca absent artificial advantages And it was apparent whom he thought ought to fund those advantages. "Let's hope there could be a 'haven' price for substitute crops" and that the United States provides more resources for the program, he said.

Putumayo's soil and climate offer no alternative crop that earns as much money as does growing coca.

Plan Colombia

The experience of Plan Colombia in one portion of Putumayo province illustrates some of the problems with the crop substitution strategy. The "carrot" portion of Bogota's carrot-and-stick approach there was a combination of economic development projects and direct financial incentives to farmers who were willing to sign pledges renouncing the growing of coca. (The "stick" was the aggressive spraying of coca crops.) At one village, Villa Garzon, people lined up to greet President Andrés Pastrana and to sign such pledges in exchange for initial payments of up to $100 per family. Many of them wore "Coca-free Putumayo" T-shirts provided by the government to highlight the president's visit.

Some peasants stated that they would honor the pledge—although whether they actually would do so over the long term was doubtful. Others were cynical from the outset. One farmer, Wilmar Ospina, told reporters bluntly that he would like to consider other crops, but he could make $10,000 a year from coca—far more than from any alternative crop and an enormous sum by Colombian standards. Indeed, the government's promised compensation (up to $870 per family in the form of tools and agricultural supplies) was less than the value of a single harvest from one hectare of coca. (To make matters even worse, the bulk of the government's meager compensation packages had yet to be disbursed by the beginning of 2002.)

Nor did the spraying campaign put small growers such as Ospina out of business. Ospina was annoyed that planes had sprayed his coca in January 2001, even though he had only five acres under cultivation and the government had promised to confine its spraying to fields at least five times that size, which authorities assumed belonged to the big drug cartels. He also echoed the complaint of many other peasants that the spraying had killed his banana plants. But Ospina also learned from the experience. By lightly washing the coca leaves shortly after fumigation and then treating them with chemicals, he was able to save a significant portion of the crop. Perhaps more to the point, within weeks he was busily planting the illicit leaf again.

Matters have not fared much better for one of Plan Colombia's showcases: a palm-heart cannery near the town of Puerto Asis. Plan money is being used to buy palm grown by local peasants switching from coca. But even local officials admit that Putumayo's soil and climate offer no alternative crop that earns as much money as does growing coca. Indeed, even outside the main coca-growing areas such as Putumayo, coca is becoming more and more prominent, sometimes displacing Colombia's most pervasive legal crop, coffee.

In a March 2002 confidential report, the U.S. State Department provided an extremely pessimistic assessment of the crop substitution component of Plan Colombia. The report concluded that farmers in southern Colombia who had signed agreements to eliminate coca in exchange for aid payments had in fact eliminated little or none of the crop, nor did they, show any intention of doing so. But what policy conclusions did U.S. officials derive from this sobering assessment? They decided to largely abandon the crop substitution scheme in favor of two other options: to intensify the aerial spraying campaign to convince Colombian peasants that their coca would be wiped out (and they would therefore suffer financial devastation) if they tried to continue growing the crop and to build large infrastructure projects to provide jobs outside of agriculture and to improve overall living conditions of people in the coca-growing areas. One would be hard-pressed to come up with two more utterly sterile proposals. Both tactics have been tried repeatedly in numerous drug-source countries in Latin America, and both have failed repeatedly to produce lasting beneficial results.

The blunt assessment of crop substitution programs made by Mexican scholar Maria Celia Toro a decade ago still applies: "No agricultural product can be made as profitable as any commodity that is to be sold on the black market. The gap between the prices of legal and illegal crops is enormous. Short of decriminalization or legalization, little can be done to eliminate the economic incentives that spur drug production and smuggling."

Attempts to Stop International Drug Trafficking Do Not Hinder the U.S. Drug Trade

John M. Walsh

John M. Walsh is senior associate for the Andes and drug policy at the Washington Office on Latin America.

Since the early 1980s, U.S. policy has sought to reduce the supply of cocaine and heroin by curbing drug production in the source countries and by seizing shipments en route. Attacking supply overseas aims to reduce the availability of illicit drugs in the United States enough to drive up prices and drive down purity. In theory, these higher prices for lower-quality product would then reduce drug use, both by dissuading people from ever becoming involved with drugs and by prompting those who are already using drugs to seek treatment or otherwise cut back on their consumption.

Until fairly recently, the conventional wisdom in the drug control field held that trying to discourage illicit drug consumption by making drugs more expensive was unlikely to accomplish much, on the assumption that heavy or frequent users of illicit drugs were not very sensitive to changes in price. However, most analysts now agree that price does matter, and that price increases, if they could be achieved, would help to reduce consumption. Demand for illicit drugs like cocaine and heroin is now considered to be somewhat elastic with respect to price, such that a 1.0 percent increase in price should reduce consumption by somewhere between 0.2 to 1.0 percent.

ONDCP's [Office of the National Drug Control Policy] 2004 *National Drug Control Strategy* asserts that the "main

John M. Walsh, "Are We There Yet? Measuring Progress in the U.S. War on Drugs in Latin America," *WOLA Drug War Monitor*, vol. 3, December 2004, pp. 6–9, 14–15. Reproduced by permission.

reason supply reduction matters to drug policy is that it makes drugs more expensive, less potent, and less available." Put more accurately, supply reduction efforts *aim* to make drugs more expensive, less potent and less available; whether such efforts succeed or not in this purpose is an empirical question that ONDCP's artful phrasing tries to evade.

Here the record is dismally clear: *Since the early 1980s, U.S. cocaine and heroin prices have actually fallen dramatically, while purity levels have risen and then remained fairly stable.* The most recent and comprehensive analysis shows U.S. wholesale and retail prices for cocaine and heroin to be at or near their historic lows, with purity at or near historic highs. The latest analysis confirms and updates previously published price and purity trends, which ran through mid-year 2000. The new time series goes through mid-year 2003, and should be of special interest to policymakers because it represents the first look at prices and purity since Plan Colombia began in 2000.

Whatever factors may account for reduced [drug] use, supply control programs are not among them.

The price-based evidence that U.S. cocaine and heroin supplies remain robust is corroborated by the Justice Department's most recent assessment of the illicit drug threat. The April 2004 report of the Department's National Drug Intelligence Center (NDIC) states:

> Both powder and crack cocaine are readily available throughout the country and overall availability appears to be stable . . . Law enforcement reporting indicates that heroin remains readily available throughout most major metropolitan areas, and availability is increasing in many suburban and rural areas, particularly in the northeastern United States.

Lack of Impact

What to make of the fact that the prices of cocaine, crack and heroin are now much lower than they were ten or twenty years ago? It would be one thing if prices had declined during a period of U.S. disinterest and disengagement from the illicit drug problem, but in fact, they dropped during a period of dramatic intensification of U.S. efforts to curtail drug supplies both at home and abroad.

Domestically, the arrest and incarceration of drug dealers has been the central feature of the stepped-up drug war, with a dramatic increase in the number of people behind bars for drug offenses, climbing from fewer than 42,000 in 1980 to more than 480,000 in 2002. This eleven-fold increase in the number of incarcerated drug offenders was nearly forty times greater than the growth rate of the U.S. population overall.

Beyond punishment for its own sake, the unprecedented recourse to incarceration has had the goal of making drugs less available by locking up sellers and deterring others from entering the market—but the relevant evidence emphatically demonstrates that it has not worked out that way. A 2003 study concludes that,

> the incapacitation effect of imprisoning a drug dealer is close to zero. Even high-level drug dealers and entire dealing organizations have proven to be replaceable, with at most, a brief interruption of supply. As long as there are drug buyers, the financial rewards of supplying their drugs will attract new organizations to replace the old.

Similarly, increased spending to control the supply of illicit drugs from overseas has not kept cocaine or heroin prices from falling. In 1981, the United States spent about $375 million on source-country drug control and interdiction. In 2004, the United States spent $3.6 billion for these same purposes, making a total of nearly $45 billion over the quarter century since 1980, more than one-third of which has been spent during the last five years (2000–2004).

An important corollary to the obvious failure to drive up cocaine and heroin prices is that reduced drug use over these past two decades cannot plausibly be attributed to source country and interdiction operations. Since prices have not risen, logic dictates that whatever factors may account for reduced use, supply control programs are not among them. For example, prior to the rise in current (past-month) cocaine use since the mid-1990s, the *National Household Survey on Drug Abuse* found that the number of current cocaine users declined from an estimated 5.7 million in 1985 to 1.5 million in 1995. Over this period, cocaine's retail price fell fairly steadily, and in 1995 the price stood at less than half its 1985 level. Clearly, the number of current cocaine users fell for reasons other than rising cocaine prices.

Enforcement can undeniably accomplish its immediate goals—e.g., eradication, seizures, arrests—but . . . the drug industry has remained intact.

Rosy Forecasts

To put it mildly, the supply-side track record does not inspire confidence—but might real success be just over the horizon? The [President George W.] Bush administration's case that we are within reach of "a major and permanent disruption of the illicit drug industry" rests largely on reported gains in terms of crop eradication, drug seizures and related indicators. Officials have predicted with apparent confidence that the increases recorded in coca eradication and cocaine seizures will translate into higher U.S. prices by mid-year 2005.

The array of indicators traditionally presented as measures of progress in international drug control—hectares of crops eradicated, tons of drugs seized, number of arrests made, and so on—undoubtedly convey a sense of action and accomplishment, and give us a sense of the pace at which overseas drug control activities are being conducted. But the number of drug control operations conducted and their immediate accomplishments do not tell us anything about whether progress has been made toward the fundamental U.S. policy goal of making supplies scarce enough to drive up cocaine and heroin prices in the United States. . . .

Unintended Consequences

Meanwhile, the pursuit of "success" as measured by the same indicators has resulted in a disturbing series of unintended negative consequences. A short list of these includes:

- a crackdown on Colombian marijuana smuggling propelled the shift from marijuana to cocaine trafficking;

- the intensification of interdiction in the Caribbean and southern Florida prompted Colombian traffickers to reroute their shipments through Mexico; and

- aggressive coca eradication and coca paste interdiction in Bolivia and Peru contributed to the expansion of coca production in Colombia.

In each case, the perceived immediate benefits were arguably outweighed by the eventual costs, even if considered strictly in terms of the new challenges facing enforcement. For example, the interdiction efforts in the Caribbean certainly compelled Colombian cocaine traffickers to move their routes out of the area, but it is difficult to consider the ensuing large-scale involvement of Mexican criminal organizations in cocaine trafficking as an advance in drug control. Similarly, tougher enforcement contributed to declining coca production in Bolivia and Peru, but the subsequent explosion of coca cultivation in Colombia has fueled the armed conflict there, even as U.S. military involvement in Colombia's counterinsurgency campaign deepens.

The traditional supply-side indicators allow U.S. drug war agencies to tout their achievements, but the indicators themselves, and the discourse they promote, divert attention from the cold reality that past successes have rearranged the drug trade, but not broken it. Enforcement can undeniably accomplish its immediate goals—e.g., eradication, seizures, arrest— but while individuals and even entire trafficking organizations come and go, the drug industry has remained intact and constantly found new ways to get illegal drugs through to consumers.

Eradicating coca actually inflicts very little damage on drug trafficking organizations and their capacity to produce and smuggle cocaine.

A False Sense of Confidence

The misplaced confidence that the traditional indicators are valid measures of success is based on a false assumption: that the activities they describe are likely to have a direct and significant impact on the ultimate retail price of cocaine in the United States. The failure to achieve such an impact to date suggests that this connection is not nearly as strong as commonly supposed. A more careful analysis of how the drug trade operates, combined with the weight of evidence regarding availability and prices, leads to the conclusion that the connection between supply side activities and U.S. cocaine and heroin prices is very weak indeed.

ONDCP asserts that the U.S. supply control strategy is based on a "market model of illegal drug production" that serves to identify "where the production chain is vulnerable to disruption." The attention lavished on drug crop cultivation and eradication figures flows from the premise that the "key vulnerability of the cocaine industry is the cultivation phase, . . ." Indeed, the State Department considers attacking drug production at the cultivation stage to be "by far the most cost-effective means of cutting supply. If we destroy crops or force them to remain unharvested, no drugs will enter the system." This is appealing in its simple logic, but unfortunately, greatly overstates the vulnerability of coca leaf to enforcement, and then compounds the error by assuming it to be a high-value target.

Drug crops are obviously susceptible to enforcement, but if they are so vulnerable, how have they eluded the knock-out blow for so long? The coca bush is a hardy and adaptable plant that flourishes on steep slopes and in acidic soils unfriendly to other crops. It requires minimal tending and yields harvestable leaves early and often: bushes are productive within a year to eighteen months after planting, and yield three to six harvests per year over a period of anywhere from ten to twenty-five years. The leaves are lightweight and durable, and well suited to low-cost, long-range transport that does not depend on access to good roads. These advantages have ensured that, in the face of enforcement pressure, coca production will persist.

The Futility of Eradication

Meanwhile, eradicating coca actually inflicts very little damage on drug trafficking organizations and their capacity to produce and smuggle cocaine. Coca leaves constitute a tiny fraction of cocaine's ultimate U.S. retail price. For less than $1,000, traffickers can purchase the coca leaf needed to produce a kilogram of cocaine that retails for about $150,000 in the United States (when sold in $100 units of one gram each, two-thirds pure). Even if the cost of coca leaf were to triple or quadruple, the impact on the ultimate U.S. retail price of cocaine would be negligible. Since traffickers' investment in their product at the initial stages of production is so minimal, it follows that attacking the drug trade at this point costs drug-trafficking organizations precious little.

U.S. drug control agencies routinely inflate the significance of their achievements by expressing the value of drug crops destroyed or drugs captured in terms of the price that the drugs might have fetched on U.S. streets. For example, the

State Department has claimed as "riveting fact" that its eradication efforts in 2001 and 2002 "took $5 billion worth of cocaine, at street value, off the streets of the United States." Such announcements imply that traffickers have been dealt a heavy blow, and that U.S. illicit drug supplies are perceptibly tighter as a result. But, as explained above, eradication takes place at a point where traffickers have invested very little, and where losses in raw materials can be recouped fairly readily or buffered against in the form of stockpiled production. A quantity of cocaine worth $5 billion on U.S. streets would be worth no more than $50 million at the cultivation stage. While eradication is indeed a heavy blow to coca farmers, traffickers' business is not jeopardized, and the disruption of production registers barely, if at all, in U.S. prices. Thus understood, the price structure of the illicit drug market makes it extremely difficult to drive up retail prices through source country programs.

Current
CONTROVERSIES

CHAPTER 2

Are Efforts to Stop Drug Trafficking Harming the United States?

Chapter Preface

The United States has more people in prison for drug-related crimes than any other country in the world. Over three hundred thousand people—around one in every thousand Americans—are currently in U.S. prisons on drug-related charges.

This number means different things to different people. To some it is a positive statistic, an indication that the United States takes its problem with illegal drugs seriously and is willing to take tough steps to confront it. From this point of view, cracking down on people who make and sell drugs is necessary to prevent drug dealers hooking kids on drugs, murdering people to protect their drug-dealing turf, and otherwise destroying communities.

On the other side, a vocal group of reformers sees the number of Americans imprisoned on drug charges as an indication that the "War on Drugs" has run amok and become a war on poor minorities, who make up a disproportionately large share of those sentenced to prison for drug-related crimes. These reformers often point to the number of scandals that have erupted in recent years over police officers framing innocent people, mostly African Americans and Mexican Americans, for drug-related crimes.

The best-known of these scandals occurred in the small town of Tulia, Texas. Forty African American residents of Tulia—well over 10 percent of the town's black population—were arrested and charged with drug offenses based solely on the testimony of a white undercover narcotics officer named Tom Coleman. Several of these defendants were convicted and given long sentences, including one who was sentenced to over four hundred years in prison, before it was discovered that Coleman had fabricated the allegations. Some of the innocent people who were framed by Coleman spent four years in jail before being exonerated and freed.

In another case, a police detective from Dallas helped to send several innocent people to jail despite knowing that the "cocaine" that was found on them was in fact ground-up pool chalk planted there by crooked informants. Outside of Texas, there have been countless cases around the country of innocent people being convicted based on the false testimony of "snitches"—criminals who were offered reduced sentences in exchange for giving police information about people involved in other crimes, particularly drug-related crimes. In many of these cases it has been alleged that the police officers should have suspected that their informants' testimony was untrustworthy or at the very least, that the officers should have tried harder to corroborate the informants' stories.

Are these isolated cases of individual police officers crossing the line or are they symptoms of a deeper problem with the entire War on Drugs? In this chapter the authors consider whether America's drug warriors are protecting Americans from the threat of drugs and drug-related crime or whether the drug warriors themselves are the bigger threat.

Banning the Sale of Drugs Increases Crime

Joel Miller

Joel Miller is a columnist and a senior editor at the Nelson Current publishing house. He is also the author of Bad Trip: How the War Against Drugs Is Destroying America, *from which the following selection is excerpted.*

Rannell Rogers is just twenty-three and makes "between $1,000 and $2,000 a week," by his accounting. But much more money is in play than his two Gs. "I worked for a guy, and I counted his money one time and for a week," said Rogers, a member of the Mafia Insane Vice Lords gang in Chicago, "counted $1.2 million sitting on my table. But it was his money. I wanted to get my gym bag and run. But he knows where my house is. That was his take."

The Black Market

Boiled down, the subject of drugs is all about cold, hard cash. There is a reason, after all, that it is referred to as the drug *trade.* Drugs are a product, just like cabbage or semiconductors; they are of no value unless people wish to buy or sell them. Realizing there is demand for chemical mindbenders is fundamental to evaluating the drug scene in America. Folks *want* to buy dope. And it is here—at the very first step—that prohibitionists begin their policy pratfall.

The idea of stamping something out by simply making it illegal ignores the role of demand in an economy. A law doesn't stop the drug buyer from buying drugs; it merely puts a fence in his way. The demand is still there, and with sufficient means and intelligence, the man will simply go around or over the fence or find a new way to slake his desire. Further, because the demand is present, suppliers, like Rogers' boss, also busy themselves figuring out ways to breach the fence and get their products to willing consumers.

The illegal meeting of the two, buyer and seller, takes place on the black market. Economist Faustino Ballvé actually calls it the "true market" because it is the only market realistically dealing with supply and demand. During any sort of prohibition, the "economic dictatorship" is "not one hundred per cent effective," he says. "The market continues to function . . . in a clandestine form." Walter Dixon, an English pharmacologist and League of Nations adviser on addiction, made note of this back in the early days of American drug prohibition: "Everything can be obtained if the price is commensurate with the risk, with the result being that smuggling is rampant from end to end in America." Likewise, said Dr. Charles E. Terry in 1920, just six years after the enactment of the United States' first federal antidrug law, the Harrison Narcotics Act, "We had counted without the peddler. We had not realized the moment restrictive legislation made these drugs difficult to secure legitimately, the drugs would also be made profitable to illicit traffickers."

Drug prohibition does not end drug use. It simply forces the consumer to break the law in order to get what he wants. And by pushing the trade into the dark corners and alleyways, prohibition sets off a string of nasty reactions.

Drugs are lucrative in a way no other product is.

Supply and Demand

The first thing that happens when drugs are forced onto the shelves of the black market is that sticker prices go up—way up. Prohibition limits supply as legal suppliers step out of the now-illegal market. The twofold, inevitable result: First, whenever demand outpaces supply, it becomes a "sellers' market," and, as any smart businessman would, the seller typically charges as much as he can get (just ask anyone trying to buy an electric generator after a hurricane strikes).

Second, prohibition increases the costs of getting the goods to market. Drug growers, producers, traffickers, and sellers all face legal sanctions for what they do. To balance that risk, the rewards must be great indeed. And they are. Between its heroin and crack sales, one New York–based drug organization in the 1990s took in about $100,000 weekly, and this was after a police crackdown hampered earnings by an estimated 20 percent—usually considered by such organizations to be little more than a tax on the trade. This is no fluke. Working just one intersection, New York police guessed that drug dealers raked in $6 million a year. Given the source of the figure, the real number might be quite higher; downplaying the count is only natural when the estimators tend to look increasingly worse in direct proportion to the size of their estimate.

Drugs are lucrative in a way no other product is. Because of government-created shortages, a grower in South America can earn three, four, even ten times the cash for growing coca (the bush from whose leaves cocaine is produced) as he can cultivating an ordinary subsistence crop. The wholesaler can peddle the cocaine in US cities for around $15,000 a kilo (2.2 pounds)—ten times what the grower makes per hectare of coca. And an ounce dealer, the final Joe in the supply chain, is sitting even prettier depending on the quality and the cut of his product. Marijuana is similar. A Mexican grower can get about $250 a kilo; for the same weight, a US seller can fetch $3,000, $5,000, and more depending on quality. Opium/heroin is the most striking. In the early 1990s, "South American drug cartels . . . discovered that growing opium poppies and refining their gum into heroin yields 10 to 20 times more profit per unit shipped than cocaine . . . heroin brings $150,000 or more [per kilo]," explained Daniel K. Benjamin in an analysis for the Independent Institute.

Instant Wealth

These high prices lure entrepreneurs into the illegal drug markets like honey draws flies. With few suppliers in the burgeoning Blow Boom of the early 1970s, profits were as mindblowing as the drug. While in prison following a major pot bust, "narcopreneur" George Jung started calculating the money he could make smuggling cocaine instead. Any thought of a legal occupation was drowned in an ocean of profit figures. The crystalline white powder, *wholesale*, was pulling prices of $50,000 and $60,000 a kilo in 1974.

"Moving from wholesaling to retailing, the numbers climbed higher still as the quality of the product got worse," writes journalist Bruce Porter in his biography of Jung. "Cut a number of times by interim dealers, who would add inert substances to boost the weight and maintain their profit margin, the common street product in some cases would contain no more than 15 or 20 percent cocaine. . . . Selling for one hundred dollars a gram, a thousand grams to the kilo, with all the deals running smoothly . . . this meant the kilo purchased for six thousand in Columbia would generate street sales in America of between two and three hundred thousand dollars. . . ."

Every 'victory' in the 'war against narcotics' increases the profitability of this trade and soon creates new pushers, more addicts, and bigger profits.

The money rolled in so fast and furiously that Jung recalled counting it became impossible. Handing a pile over to his Colombian partners, "Sometimes it was, 'Here's two and a half million dollars, and maybe it's fifty thousand off that number. I don't know.' And nobody would care. It was just,

'When can you leave and bring back more?'" The parole board thought Jung was holding down an honest job as a fisherman in Boston while all this was going on, but mackerel can't compete with that kind of mammon [wealth].

Smugglers in Jung's boat processed so much money, they often didn't count it. They weighed it. Porter explains that an even million weighs 20.4 pounds in hundred dollar bills, 40.8 in fifties. Reporter Robert Sabbag tells the story of marijuana smuggler Allen Long counting eight million dollars this way:

> The smugglers, emptying one of the cardboard boxes, placed it on the scale and came up with a tare weight. They reloaded the box, weighed it and all the other boxes, and then did the arithmetic, calculating a US banknote at precisely a gram. They came up $100,000 short, which out of $8 million-plus, fell well within the margin of error. Perhaps they overestimated the weight of the rubber bands. A hundred thousand was small change at the level at which everyone was operating. Long was spending around half that much every week in expenses.

This kind of instant wealth presents a big problem for drug warriors in inner cities. Where job prospects appear bad and hopes low, kids growing up surrounded by poverty see drug dealers rolling by in expensive cars, handing out money and favors to neighbors, and dressing well, sometimes extravagantly.

"From flashy SUVs such as the Cadillac Escalade to the fanciest clothes and jewelry, gang members show it off to command respect and lure new recruits," write *Chicago Sun-Times* reporters Carlos Sadovi and Frank Main. They mention the case of Elbert Mahone, headman of one of the Windy City's most notorious gangs. Before he was gunned down, Mahone "drove a Rolls-Royce, wore full-length fur coats and had built up a reputation as a Robin Hood for spreading money around his impoverished Lawndale community." Some of these guys are heroes on their streets, and the incredible lucre they flash and lifestyle they live draws newbies into the underground world of crime to get a piece of the action.

Crackdown

Naturally, as people rush into the market with wads of dope and loads of hope, the government steps in to crash the party. But the efforts prove counterproductive and self-defeating. "Paradoxically, every 'victory' in the 'war against narcotics' increases the profitability of this trade and soon creates new pushers, more addicts, and bigger profits," explains Peter Drucker. "When the narcotics agents 'smash a drug ring' and confiscate 50 kilograms of heroin, the drug temporarily become scarce. . . . The price goes up—and with it the profit for the drug rings whose sources remain intact. Addicts become more desperate. Crime and violence . . . rise more sharply. More people are lured by their own need and by the high profits into becoming peddlers and pushers, producing more addicts."

But this is no paradox. Shortages in supply created by crackdowns are only mating calls to suppliers. Dollar signs are fiscal pheromones. The costs may be high for suppliers, but the profits soar higher still—incentive to stay in the game (or start playing) and satisfy the demand at a price worth their while. As a result of their profit-seeking, more supply makes its way into the market, driving down prices as the shortage is slaked. Thus, what appear to be absurdly high prices are simply the way the market rations supply and encourages new supplies in response to demand. And what lucrative encouragement.

When alcohol Prohibition became law in 1920, Rev. Billy Sunday gushed with high-sounding praise. "The reign of tears is over. The slums will be only a memory. It will turn our prisons into factories and our jails into storehouses and corncribs. . . . Hell will be forever for rent."

Wrong. The government just gave Hell a housing subsidy.

Most of the drug crime people worry about . . . is a direct result, not of the pharmacological effects of dope, but of the distortion of drug markets by laws.

Prohibition Increases Crime

Prohibition creates crime in a number of ways. First, anyone who continues involvement in the once-legal trade after laws are passed against it is made a criminal—a felon not because he has harmed or defrauded his neighbors but by fiat. Other forms of crime basically break down into two groups: (1) property crimes committed by addicts to get the necessary funds to score their necessary fixes and (2) violent crimes committed by those in the trade.

In 1980 New York fell prey to a rash of necklace nabbing by train-going ne'er-do-wells, acting both alone and sometimes in packs. In one instance, after an Amtrak passenger train rammed a freight train, hoodlums ran through the cars filching gold chains and purses. The police were basically useless; the public grew fearful.

Rising above the panic and anxiety, Gov. Hugh Carey tried to make some sense of the events rippling through his crime-stricken state. "The epidemic of gold-snatching in the city," he explained in a public address, preparing to prove he had learned very little in his college Econ 101 class, "is the result of a Russian design to wreck America by flooding the streets with deadly heroin. . . . Women are afraid to walk with a chain around their neck. Why? Somebody's grabbing that chain to get enough money for a fix. . . . [If the Russians] were using nerve gas on us, we'd certainly call out the troops. This is more insidious than nerve gas. Nerve gas passes off. This doesn't. It kills. I'm not overstating the case." Or his ignorance.

Junkies commit property crimes like theft to get cash to buy a fix—that much Carey had right. But what he missed was why the fix costs so much in the first place. As the illegality of drugs inflates their prices, in many cases users are priced out of the market—at least in terms of legally acquired funds. Not able to procure enough money by methods that keep the angels smiling, some drug users turn to crime to generate the necessary greenbacks. As George Will breaks it down, "If you must steal $20 worth of property to raise $5 from a fence, then a $100-a-day habit requires $400 worth of stolen stuff." If crime were Carey's concern, then he should have been thanking the Soviets for "flooding the streets" with smack. With surpluses instead of shortages, the price would go down, thus mitigating the need to rob and pillage for a fix. The opposite is true as well. When [President Richard] Nixon vowed to crack down on drugs, it was in response to rising property crimes. However, more crackdowns mean more shortages, which create higher prices, which create more property crimes.

For those dealing in an illegal trade, contracts become enforceable with guns, not lawsuits.

This argument *can* be overstated, as drug users often do procure cash by means other than theft—including, as many addicts do, selling drugs or prostituting themselves. This by itself is troubling, since (sans prohibitionary inflation) the price of many drugs would be no more than a cup of coffee. But because of the law, people who fall into a drug habit who do not wish to harm others by stealing must instead harm themselves by whoring for drug money or risking their safety to enter the dangerous drug market to generate funds for their own habit. In a legal market, however deplorable their habit may be, they would neither have to harm others nor themselves in order to procure drugs.

What *cannot* be overstated is the breach in the wall this creates for the rest of society—a breach through which burglars pass daily. Property crimes are exacerbated by more than junkies jacking car stereos. Because limited police resources are focused on busting drug users and dealers, they are *not* making sure that uninvited guests are keeping sticky fingers off china cabinets and auto ignitions. In the 1980s, during the first major drug crackdown since Nixon, "At least 50 percent of property crime increase was due to a shift out of property crime control to drug control," explains economist Bruce L. Benson.

The federal government actually encourages this problem. Promiscuous in its dolling out of tax dollars, Uncle Sam makes funds available to state and local law enforcement. On the state side, an agency will divvy it up as best fits that state's needs. The Wisconsin Office of Justice Assistance, for instance, disburses millions of federal dollars to the state's drug-task force units. The money then goes to reimburse local agencies for overtime costs tied to drug policing—anything from traffic stops where drugs are discovered to full-throttle SWAT raids. Here's the problem: In a world of scarce resources, while you get more of what you subsidize, you also get less of what you do not. Non-drug related enforcement sees nothing of this largesse. So while busting dopers is a budgetary boon, a stake-out to nab a burglar is just a drain on the department—no doubt an uncomforting thought when one's house is robbed.

Dodging Bullets

Because of what crimes drug users actually do commit—mainly property crimes—human life is rarely endangered by them. A stolen TV set is only a material loss and a missed episode of *The Simpsons*. But the same is not true on the dealers' end, where Homer and Bart are likely to get shot in a drive-by.

Because the illegality of the drug trade removes legal protection from its participants, the business is subject to brutality. The people who thrive in the drug market are those with, as the Cato Institute's David Boaz once put it, a "comparative advantage in violence." Why? When Pfizer [a pharmaceutical company] has a problem with a client or competitor, it calls the lawyers. But for those dealing in an illegal trade, contracts become enforceable with guns, not lawsuits. Indeed, "Much of the gunfire is connected with routine practices of the drug trade, claiming territory, punishing people who do not fulfill contracts," writes Will.

Drug prohibition "encourages entry [into the market] by suppliers who are more ruthless, innovative, and have a lower regard for civility and the law," explains Walter Williams. "Pantywaist, petty, otherwise law-abiding practitioners are ousted."

A 1995 study by University of Missouri criminology professor Scott Decker confirms these observations. Using Justice Department numbers, Decker found that sellers—not cash-strapped users—are the gun-packers of the drug market. To protect his property, a drug seller is forced to go armed, since he is all the protection he is going to get. "This is an important study," said criminologist Alfred Blumstein, "because it suggests we should rethink the presumption that the pharmacological effect of drugs makes people violent and do crazy things." In the majority of cases, it's not the dope that makes people violent. It's the legal strictures themselves that encourage violence and violent participants.

Uncle Sam is not stupid about this reality. The government knows full well its policies produce violence. As noted by a 1989 US attorney general report, "the normal commercial concept of contracts, in which disputes are adjudicated by an impartial judiciary and restitution is almost always of a financial nature, is twisted, in the world of drug trafficking, into a system where the rule of law is replaced by the threat of violence."

The story was the same during Prohibition, the seedbed years of the American Mob. It was the time of the gangsters, the Mafioso, retaliatory gang warfare, and the original drive-by shooting. During Prohibition, "if I'm not exaggerating, there were about ten mobs in Chicago," one illicit liquor distributor recalled. "Of course you had to protect your territory. You couldn't call for help. If you couldn't handle it yourself, you lost it. That was the law. So when you were enfringed upon, you had to retaliate immediately, or you didn't have nothing left."

During the thirteen-year "Ignorable Experiment," property crimes ratcheted up 13.2 percent, homicide 16.1 percent, while robbery soared 83.3 percent. "Fluctuations in economic activity and major government programs . . . no doubt played some role in these statistics," explains Mark Thornton in *The Economics of Prohibition*, "but Prohibition appears to be the significant explanatory variable for changes in the crime rate. . . .

As the long blue arm of the law puts dope or drink in a hammerlock, murders increase. When the grip loosens, homicide rates slide back down. . . .

If cocaine and other drugs were legal, do you think Wal-Mart and Walgreens pharmacists would be shooting each other in the streets over turf disputes? Violence and crime have little to do with dope itself and much to do with drug *laws*.

Efforts to Stop Drug Trafficking Harm Patients with Chronic Pain

Jacob Sullum

Jacob Sullum is a senior editor at Reason, *a libertarian magazine. He is also the author of the book* Saying Yes: In Defense of Drug Use.

Under Florida law, illegally obtaining more than 28 grams of painkillers containing the narcotic oxycodone—a threshold exceeded by a single 60-pill Percocet prescription—automatically makes you the worst sort of drug trafficker, even if you never sold a single pill. Even if, like Richard Paey, you were using the drugs to relieve severe chronic pain.

Although prosecutors admitted Paey was not a drug trafficker, on April 16, [2004] he received a mandatory minimum sentence of 25 years for drug trafficking. That jaw-dropping outcome illustrates two sadly familiar side effects of the war on drugs: the injustice caused by mandatory minimum sentences and the suffering caused by the government's interference with pain treatment.

Chronic Pain Challenges

Paey, a 45-year-old father of three, is disabled as a result of a 1985 car accident, failed back surgery, and multiple sclerosis. Today, as he sits in jail in his wheelchair, a subdermal pump delivers a steady, programmed dose of morphine to his spine. But for years he treated his pain with Percocet, Lortab (a painkiller containing the narcotic hydrocodone), and Valium prescribed by his doctor in New Jersey, Steven Nurkiewicz.

When Paey and his family moved to Florida in 1994, he had trouble finding a new doctor. Because he had developed

Jacob Sullum, "Pill Sham," *Reason Online*, April 23, 2004. Reproduced by permission.

tolerance to the pain medication, he needed high doses, and because he was not on the verge of death, he needed them indefinitely. As many people who suffer from chronic pain can testify, both of those factors make doctors nervous, since they know the government is looking over their shoulders while they write prescriptions.

Unable to find a local physician who was comfortable taking him on as a patient, Paey used undated prescription forms from Nurkiewicz's office to obtain painkillers in Florida. Paey says Nurkiewicz authorized these prescriptions, which the doctor (who could face legal trouble of his own) denies.

The Pasco County Sheriff's Office began investigating Paey in late 1996 after receiving calls from suspicious pharmacists. Detectives tracked Paey as he filled prescriptions for 1,200 pills from January 1997 until his arrest that March.

At first investigators assumed Paey must be selling the pills, since they thought the amounts were too large for him to consume on his own. But the police never found any evidence of that, and two years after his arrest prosecutors offered him a deal: If he pleaded guilty to attempted trafficking, he would receive eight years of probation, including three years of house arrest.

Paey initially agreed but then had second thoughts. His wife, Linda, says he worried that he could go to prison if he was accused of violating his probation. More fundamentally, he did not want to identify himself as a criminal when he believed he had done nothing wrong. He has since turned down other plea deals involving prison time.

Unfair Prosecutions

Meanwhile, prosecutors have pursued Paey in three trials. The first ended in a mistrial; the second resulted in a conviction that the judge threw out because of a procedural error; and the third, which ended last month, produced guilty verdicts on 15 charges of drug trafficking, obtaining a controlled substance by fraud, and possession of a controlled substance.

A juror later told the *St. Petersburg Times* he did not really think Paey was guilty of trafficking, since the prosecution made it clear from the outset that he didn't sell any pills. The juror said he voted guilty to avoid being the lone holdout. He suggested that other jurors might have voted differently if the foreman had not assured them Paey would get probation.

The prosecutors, who finally obtained the draconian sentence that even they concede Paey does not deserve, say it's his fault for insisting on his innocence. "It's unfortunate that anyone has to go to prison, but he's got no one to blame but Richard Paey," Assistant State Attorney Mike Halkitis told the *St. Petersburg Times*, "All we wanted to do was get him help."

Paey's real crime, it seems, is not drug trafficking but ingratitude. "My husband was so adamant, and so strongly defending this from the very beginning, that it might have annoyed them," says Linda Paey. "They were extremely upset that he would not accept a plea bargain. They felt that anyone who had any common sense would. . . . But he didn't want to say he was guilty of something he didn't do."

The War on Drugs Harms Minorities

Jesselyn McCurdy

Jesselyn McCurdy is legislative counsel for the American Civil Liberties Union.

The American Civil Liberties Union (ACLU) would like to thank the United States Sentencing Commission for this opportunity to testify on cocaine sentencing policy and federal sentences for cocaine trafficking. The ACLU is a nonpartisan organization with hundreds of thousands of activists and members with 53 affiliates nationwide. Our mission is to protect the Constitution and particularly the Bill of Rights. Thus, the disparity that exists in federal law between crack and powder cocaine sentencing continues to concern our organization due to the implications of this policy on due process and equal protection rights of all people. Equally important to our core mission are the rights of freedom of association and freedom from disproportionate punishment, which are also at risk under this sentencing regime.

The ACLU has been deeply involved in advocacy regarding race and drug policy issues for more than a decade. The ACLU assisted in convening the first national symposium in 1993 that examined the disparity in sentencing between crack and powder cocaine, which was entitled "Racial Bias in Cocaine Laws." The conclusion more than 10 years ago of the representatives from the civil rights, criminal justice, and religious organizations that participated in the Symposium was that the mandatory minimum penalties for crack cocaine are not medically, scientifically or socially justifiable and result in a racially biased national drug policy. In 2002, we urged the Commission to amend the crack guidelines to equalize crack and powder cocaine sentences at the current level for powder cocaine. Four years later, we continue to urge the Commission to support amendments to federal law that would equalize crack and powder cocaine sentences at the current level of sentences for powder cocaine.

Background and History

In June 1986, the country was shocked by the death of University of Maryland basketball star Len Bias in the midst of crack cocaine's emergence in the drug culture. Three days after being drafted by the Boston Celtics, Bias, who was African American, died of a drug and alcohol overdose. Many in the media and public assumed that Bias died of a crack overdose. Congress quickly passed the 1986 Anti-Drug Abuse Act motivated by Bias' death and in large part by the notion that the infiltration of crack cocaine was devastating America's inner cities. Although it was later revealed that Bias actually died of a powder cocaine overdose, by the time the truth about Bias' death was discovered, Congress had already passed the harsh discriminatory crack cocaine law.

> *African Americans serve substantially more time in prison for drug offenses than do whites.*

Congress passed a number of mandatory minimum penalties primarily aimed at drugs and violent crime between 1984 and 1990. The most notorious mandatory minimum law enacted by Congress was the penalty relating to crack cocaine, passed as a part of the Anti-Drug Abuse Act of 1986. The little legislative history that exists suggests that members of Congress believed that crack was more addictive than powder cocaine, that it caused crime, that it caused psychosis and death, that young people were particularly prone to becoming addicted to it, and that crack's low cost and ease of manufacture would lead to even more widespread use of it. Acting upon these beliefs, Congress decided to punish use of crack more severely than use of powder cocaine.

On October 27, 1986, the Anti-Drug Abuse Act of 1986 was signed into law establishing the mandatory minimum sentences for federal drug trafficking crimes and creating a 100:1 sentencing disparity between powder and crack cocaine. Members of Congress intended the triggering amounts of crack to punish "major" and "serious" drug traffickers. However, the Act provided that individuals convicted of crimes involving 500 grams of powder cocaine or just 5 grams of crack (the weight of two pennies) would be sentenced to at least 5 years imprisonment, without regard to any mitigating factors. The Act also provided that those individuals convicted of crimes involving 5000 grams of powder cocaine and 50 grams of crack (the weight of a candy bar) be sentenced to 10 years imprisonment.

Two years later, drug-related crimes were still on the rise. In response, Congress intensified its war against crack cocaine by passing the Omnibus Anti-Drug Abuse Act of 1988. The 1988 Act created a 5-year mandatory minimum and 20-year maximum sentence for simple possession of 5 grams or more of crack cocaine. The maximum penalty for simple possession of any amount of powder cocaine or any other drug remained at no more than 1 year in prison.

The 100 to 1 Disparity in Federal Cocaine Sentencing Has a Racially Discriminatory Impact and Has Had a Devastating Impact on Communities of Color

Data on the racial disparity in the application of mandatory minimum sentences for crack cocaine is particularly disturbing. African Americans comprise the vast majority of those convicted of crack cocaine offenses, while the majority of those convicted for powder cocaine offenses are white. This is true, despite the fact that whites and Hispanics form the majority of crack users. For example, in 2003, whites constituted 7.8% and African Americans constituted more than 80% of the defendants sentenced under the harsh federal crack cocaine laws, while more than 66% of crack cocaine users in the United States are white or Hispanic. Due in large part to the sentencing disparity based on the form of the drug, African Americans serve substantially more time in prison for drug offenses than do whites. The average sentence for a crack cocaine offense in 2003, which was 123 months, was 3.5 years longer than the average sentence of 81 months for an offense involving the powder form of the drug. Also due in large part to mandatory minimum sentences for drug offenses, from 1994 to 2003, the difference between the average time African American offenders served in prison increased by 77%, compared to an increase of 28% for white drug offenders. African Americans now serve virtually as much time in prison for a drug offense at 58.7 months, as whites do for a violent offense at 61.7 months. The fact that African American defendants received the mandatory sentences more often than white defendants who were eligible for a mandatory minimum sentence, further supports the racially discriminatory impact of mandatory minimum penalties.

There are more African American men under the jurisdiction of the penal system than in college.

Over the last 20 years, federal and state drug laws and policies have also had a devastating impact on women. In 2003, 58% of all women in federal prison were convicted of drug offenses, compared to 48% of men. The growing number of women who are incarcerated disproportionately impacts African American and Hispanic women. African American women's incarceration rates for all crimes, largely driven by drug convictions, increased by 800% from 1986, compared to an increase of 400% for women of all races for the same period. Sentencing policies, particularly the mandatory minimum for low-level crack offenses, subject women who are low-level participants to the same or harsher sentences as the major dealers in a drug organization.

The collateral consequences of the nation's drug policies, racially targeted prosecutions, mandatory minimums, and crack sentencing disparities have had a devastating effect on African American men, women, and families. Recent data indicates that African Americans make up only 15% of the country's drug users, yet they comprise 37% of those arrested for drug violations, 59% of those convicted, and 74% of these sentenced to prison for a drug offense. In 1986, before the enactment of federal mandatory minimum sentencing for crack cocaine offenses, the average federal drug sentence for African Americans was 11% higher than for whites. Four years later, the average federal drug sentence for African Americans was 49% higher. As law enforcement focused its efforts on crack offenses, especially those committed by African Americans, a dramatic shift occurred in the overall incarceration trends for African Americans, relative to the rest of the nation, transforming federal prisons into institutions increasingly dedicated to the African American community.

The effects of mandatory minimums not only contribute to these disproportionately high incarceration rates, but also separate fathers from families, separate mothers with sentences for minor possession crimes from their children, leave children behind in the child welfare system, create massive disfranchisement of those with felony convictions, and prohibit previously incarcerated people from receiving social services such as welfare, food stamps, and access to public housing. For example, in 2000 there were approximately 791,600 African American men in prisons and jails. That same year, there were only 603,032 African American men enrolled in higher education. The fact that there are more African American men under the jurisdiction of the penal system than in college has led scholars to conclude that our crime policies are a major contributor to the disruption of the African American family.

The assertion that crack physiologically causes violence has not been found to be true.

One of every 14 African American children has a parent locked up in prison or jail today, and African American children are 9 times more likely to have a parent incarcerated than white children. Moreover, approximately 1.4 million African American males—13% of all adult African American men—are disfranchised because of felony convictions. This represents 33% of the total disfranchised population and a rate of disfranchisement that is 7 times the national average. In addition, as a result of federal welfare legislation in 1996, there is a lifetime prohibition on the receipt of welfare for anyone convicted of a drug felony, unless a state chooses to opt out of this provision. The effect of mandatory minimums for a felony conviction, especially in the instance of simple possession or for very low-level involvement with crack cocaine, can be devastating, not just for the accused, but also for their entire family.

Dispelling the Myths Associated with Crack Cocaine with Facts

The rapid increase in the use of crack between 1984 and 1986 created many myths about the effects of the drug in popular culture. These myths were often used to justify treating crack cocaine differently from powder cocaine under federal law. For example, crack was said to cause especially violent behavior, destroy the maternal instinct leading to the abandonment of children, be a unique danger to developing fetuses, and cause a generation of so-called "crack babies" that would plague the nation's cities for their lifetimes. It was also thought to be so much more addictive than powder cocaine that it was "instantly" addicting.

In the twenty years since the enactment of the 1986 law, many of the myths surrounding crack cocaine have been dispelled, as it has become clear that there is no scientific or penological justification for the 100:1 ratio. In 1996, a study published by the *Journal of the American Medical Association* (JAMA) found that the physiological and psychoactive effects of cocaine are similar regardless of whether it is in the form of powder or crack.

For instance, crack was thought to be a unique danger to developing fetuses and destroy the maternal instinct causing children to be abandoned by their mothers. During the Sentencing Commission hearings that were held prior to the release of the commission's 2002 report on Cocaine and Federal Sentencing Policy, several witnesses testified to the fact that so-called myth of "crack babies" who were thought to suffer from more pronounced developmental difficulties by their in-utero exposure to the drug was not based in science. Dr. Ira J. Chasnoff, President of the Children's Research Triangle, testified before the Sentencing Commission that since the composition and effects of crack and powder cocaine are the same on the mother, the changes in the fetal brain are the same whether the mother used crack cocaine or powder cocaine.

In addition, Dr. Deborah Frank, Professor of Pediatrics at Boston University School of Medicine, in her 10-year study of the developmental and behavioral outcomes of children exposed to powder and crack cocaine in the womb, found that "the biologic thumbprints of exposure to these substances" are identical. Dr. Frank added that small but identifiable effects of prenatal exposure to powder or crack cocaine are prevalent in certain newborns' development, but they are very similar to the effects associated with prenatal tobacco exposure, such as low birth weight, height, or head circumference.

Crack was also said to cause particularly violent behavior in those who use the drug. However, in the 2002 report on Cocaine and Federal Sentencing Policy, the Commission includes data that indicates that significantly less trafficking-related violence is associated with crack than was previously assumed. For example, in 2000: 1) 64.8% of overall crack offenses did not involve the use of a weapon by any participant in the crime; 2) 74.5% of crack offenders had no personal weapons involvement; and 3) only 2.3% of crack offenders actively used a weapon. Although by 2005 there was an increase in the percentage of crack cases that involved weapons (before the Booker decision 30.7% and after 27.8%), the assertion that crack physiologically causes violence has not been found to be true. Most violence associated with crack results from the nature of the illegal market for the drug and is similar to violence associated in trafficking of other drugs.

Mandatory penalties for crack cocaine offenses apply most often to offenders who are low-level participants in the drug trade.

Another of the pervasive myths about crack was that it was thought to be so much more addictive than powder cocaine that it was "instantly" addicting. Crack cocaine and powder cocaine are basically the same drug, prepared differently. The 1996 JAMA study found that the physiological and psychoactive effects of cocaine are similar regardless of whether it is in the form of powder or crack. The study also concluded that the propensity for dependence varied by the method of ingestion, amount used and frequency, not by the form of the drug. Smoking crack or injecting powder cocaine brings about the most intense effects of cocaine. Regardless of whether a person smokes crack or uses powder cocaine, each form of the drug can be addictive. The study also indicated that people who are incarcerated for the sale or possession of cocaine, whether powder or crack, are better served by drug treatment than imprisonment.

Federal Cocaine Sentencing Should Reflect the Original Legislative Intent of Congress and Focus on High-Level Drug Traffickers

Indeed, if the message Congress wanted to send by enacting mandatory minimums was that the Department of Justice should be more focused on high-level cocaine traffickers, Congress missed the mark. Instead of targeting large-scale traffickers in order to cut off the supply of drugs coming into the country, the law established low-level drug quantities to trigger lengthy mandatory minimum prison terms. The commission 2002 report states that only 15% of federal cocaine traffickers can be classified as high-level, while over 70% of crack defendants have low-level involvement in drug activity, such as street level dealers, couriers, or lookouts.

Harsh mandatory minimum sentences for crack cocaine have not stemmed the trafficking of cocaine into the United States, but have instead caused an increase in the purity of the drug and the risk it poses to the health of users. The purity of drugs affects the price and supply of drugs that are imported into the country. The Office of National Drug Control Policy below best explains how purity and price are related to reducing the supply of drugs.

> The policies and programs of the *National Drug Control Strategy* are guided by the fundamental insight that the illegal drug trade is a market, and both users and traffickers are affected by market dynamics. By disrupting this market, the US Government seeks to undermine the ability of drug suppliers to meet, expand, and profit from drug demand. When drug supply does not fully meet drug demand, changes in drug price and purity support prevention efforts by making initiation to drug use more difficult. They also contribute to treatment efforts by eroding the abilities of users to sustain

their habits.—National Drug Control Strategy, Office of National Drug Control Policy, The White House, February 2006, page 17.

One indication that the National Drug Control Strategy has not made progress in cutting off the supply of drugs coming into this country is the fact that the purity of cocaine has increased, but the price of the drug has declined in recent years. In the context of a business model, declining prices and higher quality products are what one would commonly expect from most legitimate products (i.e. televisions, computers and cell phones), but not from illegal cocaine trade. According to ONDCP, for cocaine from 1981 to 1996 the retail price declined dramatically and then rose slightly through 2000. However, the purity or quality of cocaine sold on the streets is twice that of the early 1980s, although somewhat lower than the late 1980s. As a result there is more cocaine available on the street at a lower price. This is a clear indication that the thrust of this country's drug control policy has not properly focused on prosecuting high-level traffickers in order to reduce the flow or drugs coming into the country.

In the 1995 Commission report on Cocaine and Federal Sentencing Policy, the Drug Enforcement Agency (DEA) explained that powder cocaine is typically imported into the United States in shipments "exceeding 25 kilograms and at times reaching thousands of kilograms." These shipments are generally distributed to various port cities across the country. In the 2002, the commission found the median quantity of drugs that importers and high-level dealers were convicted of trafficking consisted of 2962 grams of crack cocaine and 16,000 grams of powder cocaine. Even though the DEA recognizes that importers ship well over 25 kilograms at a time into the country, the discussion about what constitutes a high-level crack cocaine trafficker should at the very least start at the median level of approximately 3000 grams. We should also look to the 2002 report to begin a dialogue about the appropriate drug quantity levels for other participants in the drug trade. The 2002 report cited statistics from 2000 for median drug quantities in crack cocaine case for organizers (509g), managers (253g) and street level dealers (52g).

Increasing Support in Congress for Changing the 100 to 1 Crack Cocaine Disparity

Several members of 109th Congress introduced legislation addressing the 100 to 1 disparity between federal crack and powder cocaine sentences. Rep. Charles Rangel's (D-NY) H.R. 2456, the Crack Cocaine Equitable Sentencing Act of 2005, equalizes the drug quantity ratio at the current level of powder cocaine and eliminates the mandatory minimum for simple possession. S. 3725, the Drug Sentencing Reform Act of 2006, sponsored by Senator Jeff Sessions (R-AL) would reduce the drug quantity ratio to a 20:1 disparity by increasing the trigger level for crack and decreasing the trigger quantity amount for powder cocaine as well as change the mandatory sentence for simple possession to one year. In addition, Rep. Roscoe Bartlett (R-MD) introduced legislation that would equalize trigger quantities of crack and powder cocaine at the current 5-gram level of crack.

The ACLU strongly opposes any measures that would lower the amount of powder cocaine required to trigger a mandatory minimum. Powder cocaine sentences are already severe and increasing the number of people incarcerated for possessing small amounts of cocaine is not the answer to the problem. Additionally, any measures that decrease the amount of powder cocaine would disproportionately impact minority communities because of the disparate prosecution of powder cocaine offenses. In 2000, 17.8% of all powder cocaine defendants were white, 30.5% were black and 50.8% were Hispanics. The mandatory sentences for crack cocaine and the disparity with powder cocaine sentences have created a legacy that must come to an end.

Conclusion and Recommendations

October 2006 marked the twentieth anniversary of the enactment of 1986 Anti-Drug Abuse Act. In the twenty years since its passage, many of the myths surrounding crack cocaine have been dispelled, as it has become clear that there is no scientific or penological justification for the 100:1 sentencing disparity ratio. This sentencing disparity has resulted in unwarranted disparities based on race. Nationwide statistics compiled by the Sentencing Commission reveal that African Americans are more likely to be convicted of crack cocaine offenses, while Hispanics and whites are more likely to be convicted of powder cocaine offenses. In addition, many of the assumptions used in determining the 100:1 ratio have been proven wrong by recent data. Scientific and medical experts have determined that in terms of pharmacological effect, crack cocaine is no more harmful than powder cocaine—the effect on users is the same regardless of form. Finally, Congress made it explicitly clear that in passing the current mandatory minimum penalties for crack cocaine, it intended to target "serious" and "major" drug traffickers. The opposite has proved true: mandatory penalties for crack cocaine offenses apply most often to offenders who are low-level participants in the drug trade.

For these reasons, the ACLU urges the Commission to recommend amending the federal penalties for trafficking, distributing and possessing crack cocaine by implementing the following recommendations:

- The quantities of crack cocaine that trigger federal prosecution and sentencing must be equalized with and increased to the current levels of powder cocaine.

- Federal prosecutions must be properly focused on the high-level traffickers of both crack and powder cocaine.

- In order for judges to exercise appropriate discretion and consider mitigating factors in sentencing, mandatory minimums for crack and powder offenses must be eliminated, including the mandatory minimum for simple possession.

Innocent Convenience Store Clerks Are Being Jailed Because of the War on Drugs

Drug Reform Coordination Network

The Drug Reform Coordination Network (DRCNet) is a not-for-profit group that advocates drug legalization.

For several dozen hard-working South Asian immigrants and their families in northwest Georgia, the American dream has turned into a nightmare. Caught up in the federal government's war on methamphetamine, they now face years in prison followed by deportation for selling legal products—from cold medicine to matches to antifreeze—to undercover informants who claim they told them they were going to use the products to home cook methamphetamine.

In a case federal prosecutors call Operation Meth Merchant, a grand jury handed down indictments in June [2005] charging 49 people and 16 companies with illicitly supplying methamphetamine precursor chemicals. Of those 49 people, 47 are Indian, with many sharing the same last name, Patel. In an area of Georgia where 75% of convenience stores are run by whites, the sting almost exclusively targeted Indians. Of the 24 stores targeted, 23 were Indian-owned.

Questionable Prosecutions

The prosecutions have raised eyebrows from the beginning. According to the indictments, the informant entered the targeted convenience stores, purchased completely legal items that could be used in home meth cooking, and then made comments like "I need this to finish a cook" to store clerks.

Drug Reform Coordination Network, "Federal Meth Precursor Sting Targeting South Asian Convenience Stores Draws Protests, ACLU Intervention," *Drug War Chronicle*, January 13, 2006. Reproduced by permission.

Federal prosecutors argue that listening to such comments indicates that the clerks or store owners were thus aware that the legal products were going to be used for an illicit purpose and thus guilty of federal drug law violations punishable by up to 25 years in prison.

But there is a problem with that. Many of those indicted speak little or no English, and even the ones who do are unlikely to be up to date on the latest slang developed by methemphetamine cooks and users.

'It is . . . just ridiculous to assume that the people selling . . . products are responsible for what their customers are going to do with them.'

The sting started producing a backlash from the beginning with coverage in the *New York Times* and a call to arms from the Drug Policy Alliance last summer. The ACLU [American Civil Liberties Union] got involved in November [2005] and is now helping to represent two defendants, and industry and South Asian associations have joined the cause. But in scenes depressingly reminiscent of the early trajectory of the now infamous Tulia, Texas, drug bust, where dozens of people went to prison based on the perjured word of an itinerant undercover cop before justice was eventually achieved, some of those charged in Operation Meth Merchant have already pleaded guilty to charges they barely understood and now face years in prison followed by deportation.

"I have already watched people plead guilty to these charges, and they needed translators in court because they couldn't understand what the judge was saying," said Deepali Gokhale, campaign organizer for Raksha, a Georgia-based South Asian community association. "How are we to believe that they understood the coded slang of the undercover informant? Imagine you are in France, you barely know the language, or perhaps not at all, and someone comes up to you and starts talking in French drug slang. This is just bizarre," she told DRCNet [Drug Reform Coordination Network].

Even the judges in the cases are having to have the meth-making slang explained to them, according to court documents, leading one defense attorney, McCracken Poston, to question why immigrants with limited English language abilities were supposed to know terminology sitting judges didn't know. "They're having to tell the court what that means," Poston said. "But they're assuming that the clerks know what it means. I think in most cases they had no idea," he told the Associated Press last weekend [January 7–8, 2006].

"It is also just ridiculous to assume that the people selling these products are responsible for what their customers are going to do with them," Gokhale said. "And why were these particular stores targeted when the products they're selling are available anyway? You could find the stuff at the convenience store across the street, you can buy it at Walmart. It's more than hard to believe that people making meth are only buying the things they need at Indian-owned stores," she said.

Racial Discrimination

Gokhale was suggesting that the targeting of Indians constituted selective prosecution—prosecutions based on race or national origin—which is forbidden by the Constitution. That is what drew the attention of the ACLU, too. "There are too many unanswered questions about the validity of evidence against these store clerks for the prosecutions to go forward in good conscience," said Christina Alvarez, a staff attorney with the group's Drug Law Reform Project when it announced it was joining the case in November [2005]. "We have launched a full investigation to determine the extent of police misconduct in this ill-conceived operation."

ACLU Drug Law Reform Project attorneys this week [January 8–13, 2006] told DRCNet they could not speak to the facts in the case because they are now representing two of the defendants. But if the group is successful in arguing selective prosecution, it could result in the dismissal of charges in the case.

Federal prosecutors deny any wrongdoing and say the operation was aimed not at Indian merchants but at cracking down on the meth problem. "The United States Attorney's Office prosecutes cases based on the evidence and the law, not the defendant's race, ethnicity or last name," Patrick Crosby, a spokesman for US Attorney David Nahmias, said Sunday [January 8, 2006] in a statement. "We continue working to resolve the dozens of individual cases that are part of the Meth Merchant investigation."

Still, the case is drawing the attention of Indian organizations far beyond Georgia. "To us, anyway, this looks like an example of selective enforcement against a vulnerable immigrant community, and we are working to raise awareness of this wrong and provide support to the community," said Deepa Iyer, executive director of South Asian American Leaders of Tomorrow, a national organization dedicated to the full and equal participation of South Asians in US political and cultural life. "We've been reaching out to the South Asian community at large to provide information about what is going on and to create national awareness of these prosecutions," she told DRCNet. "Along with the South Asian Network in Los Angeles, we put out a statement to make clear this is an issue that goes beyond Georgia and affects the entire South Asian community."

"The South Asian community itself is very tightly connected, and there is a lot of solidarity," said Raksha's Gokhale. "A bunch of organizations have signed on to endorse the campaign."

Pushing Back

And now, supporters of the Meth Merchant victims have opened a new front in the struggle to quash the prosecutions.

Last Sunday [January 8, 2006], more than 300 people gathered in front of a shopping mall in Decatur, Georgia, to protest the operation. Speaker after speaker denounced the busts as discriminatory and unfair amid signs proclaiming "Stop the Prosecution!" and Hindi civil rights chants that translate to "Against every oppression and injustice, we will fight."

"We are not coming from a criminal background," Upendra Patel, president of Georgia's Asian-American Convenience Store Association, told the crowd. "We have thousands of years of culture and civilization, and we do not know what this drug is about. Putting some innocent people behind bars is not going to solve the drug problem."

"Ours is but the latest community targeted and blamed in the drug war, a war that has corrupted our institutions to the point where we are willing to send innocent people to prison for the sake of politics and creating a false sense of security," said Raksha executive director Aparna Bhattacharyya.

"It was a great rally," said Gokhale. "We had a lot of people there and got a lot of media attention, and it was really, really empowering for these people. This was our first public outcry, so we were really focused on the South Asian community, but we are working with other immigrant and people of color communities. We had several African-American speakers come out to support us, and we've gotten some support from the Latino community, but for people to come out protest anything is scary for people these days if they're not citizens. But I think we got our message out that we are not going to stand for racial targeting."

Fighting Drug Trafficking Makes the United States More Secure

Office of National Drug Control Policy

The Office of National Drug Control Policy is a part of the executive branch of the U.S. government. The office is in charge of establishing policies, priorities, and objectives for the federal government's fight against drug trafficking and use.

Domestic and international law enforcement efforts to disrupt illicit drug markets are critical elements of a balanced strategic approach to drug control. By targeting the economic vulnerabilities of the illegal drug trade, market disruption seeks to create inefficiencies in drug production and distribution, resulting in decreased drug abuse in the United States. The impact of these efforts on illegal drug use has been demonstrated by the near-disappearance of certain once-popular drugs from U.S. society. For example, after an increase in LSD use during the 1990s, the reported rates of LSD use by young people have declined by nearly two-thirds since 2001, following the dismantling of the world's leading LSD manufacturing organization in 2000. MDMA (Ecstasy) use has made a similar dramatic turnaround since U.S. law enforcement partnered with the Netherlands to disrupt several major MDMA trafficking organizations in recent years.

The effect of market disruption initiatives can also be observed in recent reductions in the level of methamphetamine use. Following State and local efforts to tighten controls on methamphetamine's key ingredients, lifetime use of methamphetamine dropped by 12 percent and the number of new methamphetamine initiates fell by 40 percent between 2004

The President's National Drug Control Strategy. Office of National Drug Control Policy, 2007.

and 2005, as measured by the most recent NSDUH [National Survey on Drug Use and Health].

Disrupting the market for illegal drugs supports additional objectives at home and abroad. Domestic legislative and law enforcement efforts have sharply reduced the production of methamphetamine in small toxic labs that posed serious hazards to many American neighborhoods. Law enforcement efforts to dismantle violent drug gangs have removed countless criminals from American streets. Internationally, U.S. drug enforcement initiatives aid American allies and further our national security interests. As highlighted in the *National Security Strategy* ... the illicit drug trade "corrodes social order; bolsters crime and corruption; undermines effective governance; facilitates the illicit transfer of weapons; and compromises traditional security and law enforcement." U.S. training, technical assistance, information sharing, and other forms of aid help allies to counter the threat of drug trafficking. In doing so, they promote security, economic development, the rule of law, and democratic governance. To achieve these goals, the United States dedicates more than $1 billion annually to international counternarcotics efforts such as those implemented by the Department of State and the Drug Enforcement Administration [DEA]. . . .

Converging Threats on the Southwest Border

Securing our borders is a top priority for the U.S. Government. The Southwest Border poses an urgent challenge to national security. A recent study by DEA's El Paso Intelligence Center [EPIC] confirms that drug trafficking organizations collect fees to facilitate the movement of all types of contraband from Mexico into the United States. These "gatekeeper" organizations control the approaches to the Southwest Border and direct smuggling—of drugs, aliens, counterfeit goods, and potentially even terrorists—into the United States. Power struggles between these organizations are responsible for widespread violence and corruption. By making headway against drug trafficking in partnership with the Mexican government, we can combat all of these serious threats to border security.

To coordinate Federal efforts to address the central position that the drug trade occupies among border threats, the [President George W. Bush] Administration has developed a *National Southwest Border Counternarcotics Strategy* and an associated *Implementation Plan*. These two documents will help guide border control efforts and will increase the emphasis on disrupting the flow of drugs into the United States and the massive backflow of illicit cash into Mexico.

The counternarcotics capabilities supporting the *National Southwest Border Counternarcotics Strategy* will be enhanced by the Department of Homeland Security's (DHS) Secure Border Initiative (SBI), a comprehensive multiyear, multithreat, border security plan that will be implemented by U.S. Customs and Border Protection (CBP). SBI will increase the number of Border Patrol agents and expand associated physical infrastructure and technology. A critical component of SBI will leverage aerial surveillance and detection sensor technology to monitor border activity. A prototype of the new border control system will be deployed along the Southwest Border in the next several months.

Central to both the *National Southwest Border Counternarcotics Strategy* and SBI is a commitment by Federal agencies to substantially increase collaboration with State, local, and tribal agencies. One example of such collaboration is the DHS-led Border Enforcement Security Task Force, which combines personnel from different Federal agencies with key State and local law enforcement agencies to target violent criminal organizations along the Southwest Border. These efforts, through the Organized Crime Drug Enforcement Task Force (OCDETF), HIDTA [High Intensity Drug Trafficking Areas] program, EPIC, the DHS-supported State and Local Fusion Centers, and other entities, combined with a continued partnership with the Government of Mexico, will enhance our effectiveness along the Southwest Border against all threats. . . .

Freezing the Flow of Drugs in the Pacific Northwest

Under the auspices of the U.S.-Canadian Integrated Border Enforcement Team program, U.S. Immigration and Customs Enforcement (ICE) officials recently led a joint investigation with authorities from the U.S. Forest Service, the U.S. National Park Service, and the Royal Canadian Mounted Police targeting a criminal organization that smuggled cocaine, marijuana, MDMA (Ecstasy), methamphetamine, and firearms across the Pacific Northwest border shared by Canada and the United States. In *Operation Frozen Timber*, investigators disrupted Canadian traffickers who used helicopters to move drugs, bulk cash, and firearms between remote areas in lower British Columbia and U.S. national park and forest lands in the State of Washington. The ultimate distribution points for the drugs smuggled in this scheme were located in western Washington and along the I-5 interstate highway corridor in Oregon and California.

As a result of the extensive intelligence, surveillance, and undercover operations in *Operation Frozen Timber*, 13 helicopters have been linked to this illicit trade, and 48 traffickers have been arrested in Canada and the United States. U.S. and Canadian authorities also have seized 860 pounds of cocaine, 8,000 pounds of high-potency "BC Bud" marijuana, 24,000 Ecstasy tablets, and 4 pounds of methamphetamine. Additionally, *Operation Frozen Timber* has yielded more than $1.5 million in U.S. currency seizures and the forfeiture of three aircraft. ICE will leverage the lessons learned in *Operation Frozen Timber* to improve counterdrug efforts in the Pacific North-

west, and will continue to work with its Canadian counterparts to freeze the drug flow across the entire northern border
of the United States.

The Production of Methamphetamine Is Dangerous and Must Be Stopped

Mark Shook

Mark Shook is the sheriff for Watauga County, North Carolina.

Methamphetamine was something we [in Watauga County, North Carolina] heard about but believed it was a far away problem; a California problem. In the spring of 2002 our 312 square mile semi-rural Western North Carolina County with a population of 48,000 full time residents was seriously impacted by the scourge of methamphetamine. We were not prepared.

I am the Sheriff of Watauga County North Carolina. I have been a professional law enforcement officer for nearly 20 years. In this time I have worked in many facets of local law enforcement. I have been a patrol officer, a detective and now Sheriff. During my years of service I have investigated murders, rapes, property crimes and even automobile crashes. Each of these significantly affect the people involved. The effect I've seen on our county from methamphetamine is not localized like these other crimes. Methamphetamine impacts in some way everyone around it.

Methamphetamine has penetrated our communities like the disease that it is.

Harm to Children

It is our families that are hardest hit. Methamphetamine addicts do not hold jobs; they do not contribute to our society. *These individuals are users, plain and simple.* They use our

Mark Shook, "Testimony of Mark Shook, Sheriff of Watauga County, North Carolina," *Hearing Before the Subcommittee on Criminal Justice, Drug Policy, and Human Resources, U.S. House Committee on Government Reform*, July 26, 2005. Reproduced by permission of the author.

community's resources; they steal from their family members. They break into their neighbors houses. They become physically aggressive to those around them, often to people they love; even their children. Finally, they rob and kill because of perceived needs and paranoia.

So many times we have seen first hand the hardest hit victims are the defenseless; the young children who are forced to live in conditions that are appalling by any standard. Time and again we've raided active clandestine methamphetamine laboratories and found children living in these contaminated structures. We've seen baby bottles soaking in a sink full of chemical waste from methamphetamine production. I have taken teenagers from their parents' methamphetamine lab and found coffee filters with wet methamphetamine in their pockets; fresh from a methamphetamine "cook." I spoke with a six-year-old boy who lived with his mother and father in a methamphetamine laboratory. This six-year-old told me step by step the process his mom and dad used to manufacture methamphetamine; *step by step*. This child's parents had used him many times to assist them in cooking methamphetamine.

Many . . . amateur methamphetamine cooks have been badly burned while trying to cook methamphetamine.

In January of this year [2005] two small children were abducted at gunpoint from a foster home in Watauga County by their biological parents. The children were in protective custody because their parents were operating a methamphetamine laboratory in their house. These methamphetamine addicts found out where their children were housed, got a pistol, drove there and held the foster family at gunpoint while they took the children. Four days, an Amber Alert, and one car chase later we recovered the children, thankfully unharmed, in our neighboring state of Virginia. The parents were immediately arrested and searched. Again, they were carrying methamphetamine. The children are now back in foster care and the parents are in jail awaiting trial on kidnapping, armed robbery, and methamphetamine manufacturing charges.

Threats to Public Safety

In our small county we have had methamphetamine related homicides, robberies, and sex offenses. In a county where murders are few and far-between, most of the murders that have occurred in our county recently have had various ties to methamphetamine. Houses, mobile homes and apartments have burned due to the flammability and toxicity of the chemical mixtures people use while trying to manufacture methamphetamine. Many of these amateur methamphetamine cooks have been badly burned while trying to cook methamphetamine.

Clandestine methamphetamine laboratories represent the single greatest threat to the safety of emergency responders in our county. I have officers in my department that have been injured investigating meth labs. Six volunteer firefighters from one department in our county have been injured, one seriously and permanently while working to extinguish meth lab related fires. These injuries are not from the fire itself, nor a fall; these injuries are from the toxic fumes produced by the methamphetamine cooking process. We have been lucky in Watauga County, North Carolina. None of our responders have been killed, but around the country firefighters, medics, law enforcement officers, and many others in the public safety/ public service industry are seriously injured or killed every year from on the job exposure to these clandestine laboratories.

I was elected Sheriff in 2002. Before my election I was a detective at the Sheriff's Office. In the year before I took office I noticed a trend developing in cases I was investigating. I kept hearing the word "Meth." I was vaguely aware of methamphetamine from training and word of mouth but I really didn't know much about it. What I did know was that "meth" was being identified with more and more criminal activity. A murder I worked earlier in the year turned out to be a meth lab dispute, suspects in sexual assault cases were citing methamphetamine as a contributing factor in their behavior. I came to understand that our community was suddenly awash in methamphetamine.

Fighting Meth

I saw first hand the damage resulting from people using this drug. I knew we had to take action and we did. We began an aggressive campaign against methamphetamine and the people producing it. Some eighty meth labs later officers in my department can point to tremendous successes. We have been instrumental in the passage of state laws that provide enhanced punishment for meth producers; we have made many arrests that led to our serious meth producers receiving sentences ranging from state probation to more than forty years in federal prison.

It is now difficult to find a clear cut methamphetamine lab in our county. There are still a few in operation and we're closing in on those. We do find "dump sites" where lab related materials are illegally dumped but these too have declined. We have worked hard to deter people from manufacturing methamphetamine and to make it more difficult to get the necessary materials. We have worked to educate our citizens and we have developed relationships with our retailers. We established a three county meth task force dedicated to the investigation and seizure of meth labs and arresting those responsible for their operation. We are continually fighting the methamphetamine epidemic. Even with these efforts and the success we have had the use of methamphetamine is still prevalent in our area. We believe the majority of it is being brought in from the Western states and Mexico.

We are fighting a battle; working everyday to rid our county of methamphetamine and we are doing a good job; but we need help. We need laws passed controlling the sale of pseudoephedrine; the necessary ingredient for meth production. States such as Oklahoma have passed legislation making it very difficult for meth producers to purchase or steal large amounts of pseudoephedrine. Laws controlling the over-the-counter sale of pseudoephedrine have had a significant impact and have contributed to a substantial drop in methamphetamine production in the states passing them. North Carolina is considering similar laws but they have not [been] adopted. The passage of federal legislation controlling sales of pseudoephedrine would have the single biggest impact on illicit methamphetamine producers. . . .

Clandestine methamphetamine laboratories have moved east for some years now and have made it all the way across the country. They are a local problem, a state problem, and now most of all, a national problem.

Doctors Who Treat Chronic Pain Patients Do Not Need to Fear the War on Drugs

Karen P. Tandy

Karen P. Tandy is the head of the U.S. Drug Enforcement Administration.

Today [September 6, 2006] DEA [Drug Enforcement Administration] has good news for people in chronic pain who need medication to control their pain and bad news for those who divert these drugs.

At noon today, DEA will be announcing 2 new steps that we are taking to ensure that people who medically need drugs get them, and that those who are diverting them, don't:

- First, we're proposing new regulations that will make it easier for doctors to prescribe Schedule II drugs for chronic conditions.

- Second, we're issuing a first of its kind policy statement to give the medical community the information they requested on prescribing and dispensing controlled substances to treat pain.

- Third, we are launching a new page on our website to provide everyone with the facts on DEA cases against doctors who violate federal drug laws.

These are all firsts.

Before I get into each of these, let me tell you how we got here.

Prescription Drug Abuse

We all know that prescription drugs help millions of Americans every day, including those who suffer from chronic pain.

Karen P. Tandy, "Dispensing Controlled Substances for the Treatment of Pain," *Drug Enforcement Administration, U.S. Department of Justice*, September 6, 2006.

When it works right, they get desperately needed relief. Taken outside of medical necessity, these drugs can and do kill.

- Today, more than 6 million Americans are abusing prescription drugs—that is more than the number of Americans abusing cocaine, heroin, hallucinogens, and inhalants, combined.

Think about that number—6 million is a huge number of people—it would be the equivalent of the combined population of Chicago, Houston, and Philadelphia.

- If we look at the people who are just starting out as new drug users, prescription drugs have overtaken marijuana and cocaine as the drug of choice.

- Most parents don't realize that nearly 1 in 10 high schools seniors admits to abusing powerful prescription painkillers, specifically Vicodin.

- And finally, opioid painkillers now cause more drug overdose deaths than cocaine and heroin, combined.

Some teens and adults ask what harm can a prescription high do? The families of Jason Surks in New Jersey and Ryan Haight of California know the harm. Their 19- and 18-year-old sons overdosed and died from prescription narcotics that they bought over the Internet. Neither of these boys—not Jason or Ryan—imagined that prescription drugs would kill them. People need to know how deadly this kind of abuse is.

It's DEA's job to enforce the federal drug laws that were enacted to protect the public from this very danger.

Drug-Dealing Doctors

Doctors practice medicine. DEA simply enforces the law to ensure that controlled substances don't end up in the hands of abusers and traffickers.

And these abusers get prescription drugs from a whole host of sources: from the Internet, burglary, theft, and stealing from pharmacies, doctor shopping to collect pain pills, and some are just forging their prescriptions.

Unfortunately, a small number of unscrupulous doctors are also illegally supplying those drugs. Although there are very few of them, they are doing tremendous damage. One such doctor in Panama City, Florida, was diverting so many OxyContin pills to abusers and traffickers that after DEA arrested him, the street price of OxyContin nearly doubled in the area because of the significantly diminished availability of OxyContin.

These are the doctors DEA investigates—ones who knowingly and egregiously put drugs into the hands of traffickers and abusers.

This isn't just questionable behavior. There is no gray area here. It's a clear cut violation of criminal law.

Last year was the largest number of doctors we arrested at 62, but it was still less than 1/10th of 1%. So far this year, we've arrested 31.

Helping Chronic Pain Patients

DEA's responsibility to enforce the law, however, does not diminish our firm commitment to the balanced policy of promoting pain relief and preventing the abuse of pain medications.

To make sure we get it right, we have spent considerable time:

- Meeting with representatives from the medical community, treatment providers, pharmacists, state pharmacy and medical boards and prosecutors, and

- Listening to the comments of more than 600 medical professionals, patients, and others affected by chronic pain and other chronic conditions.

We are convinced—I am personally convinced—that after this careful and thorough process—DEA has stayed in our lane under the law, that we have stayed out of the practice of medicine, and that the new steps we are taking today are the most effective way to strike that critical balance between promoting pain relief and preventing the diversion and abuse of powerful prescription drugs. . . .

First, we are proposing a new rule that, if it becomes final, will permit doctors to issue multiple Schedule II prescriptions during a single office visit, allowing patients to receive up to a 90-day supply of controlled substances according to the fill date that the doctor gives the pharmacist.

The law prohibits refilling powerful Schedule II controlled substance prescriptions but the regulations that implement the statute did not address the issuance of multiple prescriptions. There was silence in the regulations on this.

We heard from hundreds of doctors and patients about the burdensome requirement of repeated visits to a doctor's office each month to get a new prescription for an already diagnosed chronic condition such as Attention Deficit and Hyperactivity Disorder or chronic pain.

We hope to fix that . . . which is why we are proposing a new regulation.

Cases Against Doctors

Second, we are publishing in the *Federal Register* today, a first of its kind policy statement that answers doctors' questions about dispensing pain meds and the laws DEA must follow. . . .

Next, some doctors say that they fear DEA enforcement, so much so that they no longer prescribe pain medication. But the fact is, that less than 1/10th of 1% of the more than 770,000 DEA physician registrations in our country are revoked in any given year. Only 12% of the doctors investigated by DEA in 2005 were pain specialists.

Last year was the largest number of doctors we arrested at 62, but it was still less than 1/10th of 1%. So far this year, we've arrested 31.

So, to give doctors the comfort level to prescribe all medically appropriate pain relief to their patients without fear of enforcement action, today we are launching an innovative new page on our website, www.dea.gov, called "Cases Against Doctors," which lists the public facts from our cases against doctors.

With this new webpage, everyone, including doctors, will see the limited number of doctors we take action against and what causes us to initiate these cases. Most were referrals from state medical boards or their peers.

Law-abiding physicians will see that doctors on this webpage engaged in criminal activity that 99% of doctors wouldn't even dream of committing.

What you'll see is that:

- We stopped doctors who sell medically unnecessary prescriptions for cash.

- Doctors who exchange narcotics for sexual favors.

- Doctors who write prescriptions to make-believe patients so that the drugs could be sold on the street.

- Doctors who prescribed vast quantities of drugs to patients who admitted outright that they were re-selling the medicine. It is astonishing, but these patients have even tested positive for illegal drugs, have had needle tracks up and down their arms, and yet they were still getting these powerful painkillers.

- And, finally, we stopped doctors who have written prescriptions to patients and then require the patients to give the doctor some or all of the pills for the doctor's use, to feed the doctor's own addiction.

To start with, this new webpage reports all of DEA's administrative cases against doctors since 2003 and 25 of the criminal cases that were concluded by trial or guilty pleas. These were the first easy ones to begin posting.

Over the next 90 days, we expect to gather the balance of the criminal case records and publish the facts of the remaining cases against doctors on the webpage, and then continuously thereafter update the website with any new cases. This website is the first time this has ever been done; it is the first time a law enforcement agency has posted what caused them to initiate the case. . . .

Finally, to help doctors understand their shared responsibility to prevent diversion and abuse. DEA also has updated our *Practitioner's Manual* and posted it on our website today. Beforehand, DEA asked a number of doctors to review this manual, which updates the earlier 1990 edition, and the doctors found the new edition to be very helpful in understanding their legal obligations in prescribing drugs and the process.

The bottom line is this—Doctors need to practice medicine as they have been trained to do and what they are sworn to do: to help their patients by delivering all medically necessary pain relief. And DEA will do what we are sworn to do: enforce our nation's laws to ensure drugs are used only for the health and welfare of the public—and to ensure that these drugs don't feed addictions, or ruin innocent lives.

CHAPTER 3

How Does the War on Drugs Affect Latin America?

Overview: The War on Drugs in Latin America

Michael Shifter

Michael Shifter is an adjunct professor at Georgetown University and vice president for policy with Inter-American Dialogue.

In the popular imagination, the drug issue in Latin America is inextricably tied to the Andean region and, in particular, Colombia. Colombia produces over 90 percent of the cocaine consumed in the United States from its approximately 144,000 hectares of coca fields.

Colombia

Moreover, of all the Andean countries—indeed in all of Latin America—Colombia is most in sync with the anti-narcotics approach advocated by Washington. Over the years there have been differences and disagreements on a variety of questions, particularly related to the sensitive issue of extradition. But, beginning with the administration of Andrés Pastrana (1998–2002), when the multiyear antidrug aid package known as Plan Colombia was backed by the [President Bill] Clinton administration and approved by the US Congress, Washington and Bogotá have converged on drug policy. Since Plan Colombia was launched in 2000, the United States has provided Colombia with over $4 billion in mostly antidrug, military, and police assistance. Outside of the Middle East, Colombia is the largest recipient of US security aid.

Just a few years ago the country was commonly depicted as a "failed state." Today [2007] that characterization is inapt. US aid has certainly helped stem the deteriorating conditions in Colombia and enabled the government to reassert its au-

Michael Shifter, "Latin America's Drug Problem," *Current History*, vol. 106, February 2007, pp. 59–63. Copyright © 2007 by Current History, Inc. Reprinted with permission from Current History magazine.

thority. Particularly during the first years of the Alvaro Uribe administration, which began in 2002, the reductions in killings and kidnappings were impressive by any measure, contributing to greater confidence and optimism among most Colombians. Thanks in part to more military equipment and training, the state improved its capacity to protect Colombian citizens.

At the same time, however, it is hard to make the case that Plan Colombia has succeeded in reducing the drug problem—in Colombia, the wider region, or the United States. The results are particularly dismal when viewed in relation to the huge cost invested in the antidrug effort. Even the focal point of eradication programs in the Putumayo region of southern Colombia has witnessed meager gains overall. Current policy instruments are simply unable to match the power of market forces; coca may be effectively eradicated in one area, only to pop up in another. This so-called balloon effect can be seen within Colombia and the Andean region as a whole. Even when one country registers a success, it is often offset by a neighbor's setbacks.

The Colombian experience since the early 1980s suggests that any economic benefits that might be derived from the drug trade are significantly outweighed by its negative, often devastating consequences. The human toll in terms of deaths attributable to the drug problem—at all levels of Colombian society—has been incalculable. The country's three principal armed groups, the Revolutionary Armed Forces of Colombia (FARC), the National Liberation Army (ELN), and the paramilitary forces, are substantially involved in the drug business—including thousands of militants who have been recently demobilized. The revelations in late 2006 of the deep infiltration by para-military groups into Colombia's political system have triggered a growing scandal and illustrate the magnitude and gravity of the problem. Corruption affecting the public sector and private organizations is profound. The gains made in enhancing state authority risk reversal unless serious steps are taken to contain the spreading crisis and to clean up Colombia's sullied politics.

Ecuador

While each of Colombia's neighbors has felt the effects of that country's battle with illegal armed groups, Ecuador has been the most vulnerable to Colombia's eradication efforts, particularly the fumigation of coca crops. The border between the two nations is extremely porous, and there have been spillover effects—refugees and violence—from the implementation of Plan Colombia. There is also a serious dispute about the health and environmental impact of the glyphosate used in spraying the coca.

Ecuador's new president, Rafael Correa, has taken a particularly adamant stand against crop fumigation, a position that has broad appeal among Ecuadorans who believe their country has been unnecessarily dragged into the Colombian conflict, with little compensation for their contribution and sacrifice. Indeed, Correa, reflecting Ecuadoran public opinion and invoking the principle of sovereignty, has made it clear that he will not renew the lease with the United States for its anti-narcotics base in the coastal town of Manta when it expires in 2009. Although its coca production is negligible, Ecuador serves as a key transit point—a record 45 metric tons of cocaine were seized at the border in 2005—and thus suffers consequences reflected in institutional corruption and associated violence.

Venezuela

Venezuela, too, is not a drug-producing nation, yet it is hardly immune to the wider problem. The government of Hugo Chávez denied charges made in December 2006 by the US ambassador in Caracas, William Brownfield, that over the past decade drug trafficking through Venezuela has grown tenfold.

Mirroring wider distrust and antagonism in the bilateral relationship, there has been virtually no cooperation between the Venezuelan and US governments on the drug problem since early August 2005, when Chávez accused US drug-enforcement agents of espionage. In recent years common crime has jumped considerably; Venezuela now has the highest rate of killings by guns in all of Latin America. Although the skyrocketing level of crime is not entirely drug-related, some of the violence can be traced to the widespread availability of drugs and the growing presence of organized trafficking operations.

Bolivia

Along with Colombia, Bolivia and Peru are the main coca-producing countries in Latin America. Both have extensive cooperation programs with the United States focused on eradication and interdiction. In Bolivia, the first year [2006] of the [Evo] Morales government has seen stepped-up cocaine interdiction efforts and implementation of a cooperative coca reduction approach in the Chapare region. But the armed forces still play a front-line enforcement role criticized by some rights groups. Moreover, the successes in Chapare will be hard to repeat in other coca-growing areas. For political reasons, Morales has to move cautiously and remain sensitive to the coca growers who represent a pillar of his political base. Despite some predictable friction with the United States regarding Morales's coca-versus-cocaine distinction, an eventual accommodation on drug policy between Washington and La Paz remains a possibility.

> *More than 2,000 Mexicans were killed in drug-related incidents nationwide last year.*

Peru

Peru's acute and pervasive crime problem can be attributed in some measure to the production, trafficking, and consumption of illegal drugs. In 2006, Ollanta Humala, a former military official, campaigned for president on a law-and-order platform, winning the first round and garnering nearly 48 percent of the vote in the second. Sensing hardening public opinion and wanting to send a message, [Alan] Garcia in one of his first acts as president pushed for the death penalty for those convicted of terrorism. Garcia framed his proposal as a response to the resurgence of the Shining Path movement. Although it no longer poses a strategic threat to the Peruvian state, the group continues to be active and problematic, as evidenced by its brutal ambush and murder of five police officers and three civilians in Ayacucho in December 2006—and it is buttressed by links to drug trafficking and production. The sentencing of Peru's former national security chief, Vladimiro Montesinos, to life in prison for massive corruption during the 1990s, closely tied to drug trafficking operations, underscores the corrosive impact of drugs on governance and institutions.

Mexico

Although the commonly invoked term "Colombianization" may distort more than it clarifies given the particularity of each situation, there is little question that Mexico's drug-related problems of violence and corruption have acquired greater urgency and now rank as top priorities on the country's political and public policy agendas. It is notable that, shortly after [Felipe] Calderón assumed the presidency on December 1 [2006], he undertook a bold offensive against drug traffickers in his home state of Michoacán. The president dispatched nearly 7,000 federal forces to deal with feuding gangs responsible for some 500 murders in 2006 alone. More than 2,000 Mexicans were killed in drug-related incidents nationwide last year [2006] a big jump from 2005. Whether or not Calderon's move will prove effective, it was a clear measure of his decisiveness and his responsiveness to Mexico's increasingly intolerant attitudes toward unchecked drug-related violence. This approach contrasts sharply with the perceived inaction of the preceding Vicente Fox administration on this potent issue.

Mexico is the transit route for roughly 70 percent to 90 percent of the illegal drugs entering the United States.

Most Mexican specialists who track drug-related security challenges are far from sanguine about conditions improving, at least in the short term. They point to the growing strength, proliferation, and fragmentation of the country's myriad drug traffickers, making them much harder to contain, along with the insufficient resources and instruments at the disposal of the Mexican government to deal effectively with the problem. In addition, there are serious reservations over whether Mexico's military or police forces should take the lead in combating the well-armed drug traffickers. While many argue that this is properly a police function and that mobilizing the military carries risks for abuse, others maintain that the police are thoroughly corrupt, unreliable, and ill-equipped to handle increasingly violent traffickers. In 2001, Mexico's attorney general fired more than 1,400 federal officers for their involvement in the drug trade. In either case, the state's limited capacity—in both resources and institutions—is striking. As in Colombia and elsewhere, despite the admirable and often tremendously courageous efforts of judges, prosecutors, mayors, law enforcement officials, and journalists, the drug problem tends to penetrate and debase Mexico's public and private institutions.

The connections between Mexico's drug-related difficulties and the United States are many and profound. For starters, Mexico is the transit route for roughly 70 percent to 90 percent of the illegal drugs entering the United States. Without America's strong appetite for illegal drugs it is doubtful Mexico would be forced to wage such a battle. In addition, traffickers can easily obtain weapons such as AK-47s, most of which are smuggled from the United States. Along the US-Mexico border, the kidnapping trade, closely tied to the drug trade, is flourishing. Officials maintain that Americans now have the same chance of getting abducted on the US side as in notoriously dangerous Mexican border towns like Nuevo Laredo. But the United States, lax in controlling the illegal arms trade, cannot afford to scold Mexico for not doing its part in addressing its public safety problem. Nor can the United States afford to adopt hard-line and symbolically offensive measures aimed at controlling immigration, such as constructing a wall along the border. Such unwarranted and counterproductive responses erode the good will and mutual confidence that are essential to tackling a grave and shared challenge.

Central America's Struggles

Perhaps even more dramatic than the Mexican case are the experiences of the Central American and Caribbean countries, many of which have weak states and are struggling to deal with severe strains that often stem from the drug trade. In Central America, the civil wars have ended, but the problem of physical insecurity—aggravated by the availability of arms—persists, and may even be more acute than before. The politically motivated violence that wracked Central America in the 1980s has been replaced by burgeoning criminality at many levels, including transnational and local, much of it a product of illegal drug trafficking.

Guatemala, Central America's largest country, reached a peace agreement with guerrillas a decade ago, but its government today is woefully ill-equipped to keep rampant criminality in check. Much of the violence reportedly derives from what are often referred to as "dark forces" or "parallel powers" that have transnational connections, are sometimes linked with the country's security services, and are often involved in the drug trade. Large cocaine and heroin deliveries enter Guatemalan ports via speedboats and fishing vessels, then are broken down into smaller shipments and sent over land to the United States via Mexico. Traffickers are often paid in drugs, which then enter the domestic market and contribute to the rise in common crime, a related but distinct phenomenon afflicting the country. Polls show that public opinion in Guatemala, as elsewhere, is decidedly in favor of tougher measures—"zero tolerance" platforms are popular—to deal severely with violent criminals.

> *The small states of the Caribbean are especially vulnerable to being overwhelmed by drug-related activities.*

Central America's Maras

Guatemala has some of the gangs or "maras" (the term comes from *marabunta*, a plague of ants that devours everything in its path) that are estimated to have roughly 100,000 members in Central America alone. But the influence of these groups is most pronounced and troubling in El Salvador. The homicide rate there has soared, increasing by 25 percent between 2004 and 2005 alone, making it among the highest in the world. Here, too, public security forces have been unable to deal with the spreading problem. El Salvador's gangs are heavily involved in the drug trade, acting as enforcers and dealers within established distribution networks, creating their own inroads and supply chains, and using profits and addiction to recruit new members.

The mara problem, particularly in El Salvador, is closely tied to the immigrant experience in the United States, where young Salvadoran males first became involved with gangs and then were deported. In Honduras, too, the maras and pervasive insecurity pose one of the most difficult tests for the new government of Manuel Zelaya. In Nicaragua, Costa Rica, and Panama, the gang problem and drug-related violence are less severe, but all three countries serve as transit points for drug shipments to the United States, a fact that poses a significant threat to democratic governance.

The Caribbean

The small states of the Caribbean are especially vulnerable to being overwhelmed by drug-related activities. Just as the "balloon effect" functions when law enforcement agencies try to eradicate coca production, traffickers frequently switch their routes to avoid authorities when interdiction efforts are concentrated in a particular area such as Central America. Given access to technology and ample financial resources, drug traffickers are remarkably mobile and adaptive, representing as such the dark side of globalization. Caribbean islands, particularly the Bahamas, Jamaica, Cuba, and Hispaniola, are often used to traffic drugs to the United States and Europe. Money laundering and the inevitable, attendant corruption are also widespread in a number of Caribbean countries, where weak governmental authorities have difficulty exercising effective control. Some Caribbean nations—Jamaica, for example—have also witnessed high levels of criminal violence, some of which is drug-related, along with considerable drug consumption.

For US policy, and particularly the Miami-based US Southern Command, Central America and the Caribbean's burgeoning mara problem and patterns of drug trafficking are of utmost concern. Unfortunately, few instruments and resources are available to help bolster structures of governance and repair the frayed institutional and social fabric in these countries. The emphasis, instead, is on law enforcement, with support for police and military forces. Police forces, however, typically lack professional training and are seldom capable of dealing with such potent—often well-funded, well-organized, and well-armed—illegal forces. And, in view of Central

America's recent history with civil conflict and human rights violations, relying on the armed forces carries enormous risks of backsliding.

Brazil

Brazil's institutional capacity and resources far exceed those of the smaller Central American and Caribbean states. Yet, in looking ahead to [Luiz Inácio] Lula [da Silva]'s second term as president, one of the most troubling factors—and a potential source of instability—is the rampant insecurity in the country's major cities, where homicide is the leading cause of death among 15- to 24-year-olds. The drug trade fuels much of this violence. In Rio de Janeiro, for example, gang warfare is the norm. Some have characterized daily life in the city's *fayelas* (shantytowns), where 17 percent of Rio's citizens live, as resembling a civil war. Most of the violence, studies show, can be tied to either obtaining or using drugs. Sa;ato Paulo has also witnessed high levels of violence, largely as a result of the introduction of crack and powder cocaine. Drug dealing and drug use now account for approximately 20 percent of the city's murders. The First Command of the Capital (PCC) has evolved into a particularly formidable and brutal criminal organization, in part sustained by drug trafficking, that operates out of Sa;ato Paulo's prisons.

In recent years, drug consumption in Brazil has increased substantially. Brazil is currently the second-largest consumer of cocaine in the world, after the United States (together, the two countries account for roughly half of the cocaine consumed globally). Consumption patterns affect all socioeconomic levels. At the same time, Brazil remains a major transit country for drugs shipped chiefly to Europe. Some 90 tons of cocaine enter Brazil each year, and approximately 40 tons—15 percent of total South American cocaine exports—are sent abroad. Sa;ato Paulo has become a particularly significant export center and a hub for complex transnational drug trafficking and money-laundering networks.

Like other Latin American leaders, Lula is under enormous pressure to adopt tough measures to contain the spreading criminality. Apart from the public health dimensions of the crisis, the drain on already strapped institutions, and the corruption effect, there is a risk that deepening insecurity could dampen tourism and foreign investment rates. This, in turn, would jeopardize the prospect for economic growth and redistribution of resources, a central goal of the Lula government. In his first term Lula showed little reluctance to call on the armed forces, when necessary, to quell unrest and keep order in major urban centers. Lula's success in his second term—critical for broader, regional progress and the standing of Latin America as a whole—will hinge on his ability to get the drug problem under better control.

The Southern Cone

Even beyond Brazil, the effects of the drug trade are increasingly unmistakable in Southern Cone countries. As the market responds to shifts and pressures, for example, Argentina has started to play a more important role in the production and transshipment of cocaine—much of it directed to Europe, as the US market becomes saturated. From 1999 to 2003, just eight laboratories were found in Argentina, whereas twelve were discovered in 2004 alone. The consumption of "paco" (cocaine base paste) in cities like Buenos Aires [Argentina] and Montevideo [Uruguay] has exploded in recent years. Chile, too, has seen an increase in cocaine and marijuana consumption and has also been the source of precursor chemicals used in Peru and Bolivia. For new and fragile democratic governments like Paraguay's, the impact of the drug problem—connected to an array of other illicit activities—is of particular concern.

The War on Drugs Harms Human Rights and Democracy in Mexico

Laurie Freeman and Jorge Luis Sierra

Laurie Freeman is a fellow at the Washington Office on Latin America. Jorge Luis Sierra is a journalist with Mexico City's El Universal *newspaper.*

The links between U.S. counterdrug policy and Mexico's human rights problems and fragile democracy are difficult to disentangle. Mexico had a dismal human rights record long before U.S. drug control policy took hold, and Mexican presidents have frequently experimented with militarizing police and law enforcement institutions, often in response to their own citizens' clamor for a tough-on-crime approach. Yet by fueling the Mexican military's intrusion into police work, by supporting police units and forces that are not transparent or accountable, and by applying a scorecard approach to drug control, U.S. drug control policies have adversely affected Mexico's human rights situation.

Police Brutality

The State Department itself has recognized that "the police and military were accused of committing serious human rights violations as they carried out the Government's efforts to combat drug cartels." In the 1970s, as part of Operation Condor, the Mexican government sent 10,000 soldiers and police to a poverty-stricken region in northern Mexico plagued by drug production and leftist insurgency. Hundreds of peasants were arrested tortured, and jailed, but not a single big drug

Laurie Freeman and Jorge Luis Sierra, "Mexico: The Militarization Trap," *Drugs and Democracy in Latin America: The Impact of U.S. Policy*, ed. by Coletta A. Youngers and Eileen Rosin. Boulder, CO: Lynne Rienner Publishers, 2005. Copyright © 2005 by Lynne Rienner Publishers, Inc. All rights reserved. Reproduced by permission.

trafficker was captured. During the [President Carlos] Salinas administration [1988–1994], a U.S.-supported counter drug brigade within the judicial police was implicated in the worst reports of torture and killing, including the Norma Corona assassination. The elite brigade was composed of many police officers that had previously served in earlier repressive police units. During [President Ernesto] Zedillo's term [1994–2000], antidrug police and soldiers were responsible for scores of forced disappearances in drug-trafficking centers such as Juárez and Culiacán. In some cases the police and soldiers had been hired by traffickers to eliminate enemies; in other cases they had arrested, interrogated, and presumably tortured the victims before they disappeared. Abuses committed by soldiers and police during counterdrug operations continue[d] under the [President Vicente] Fox administration [2000–2006].

The Mexican military has committed a range of human rights violations in the context of antidrug efforts.

Alarming allegations of torture and corruption surfaced within the Federal Investigations Agency [AFI] as well. Only six months after AFI's creation, detainee Guillermo Vélez Mendoza was killed while in the custody of AFI agents. After the National Human Rights Commission determined that Vélez died as a result of torture, the agent implicated in his death was arrested, but he escaped after being released on bail. By the end of the year [2002] no AFI agent was being held accountable for Vélez's death. The practice of using *madrinas* [thugs hired as freelance policemen] has not disappeared with the AFI. In June 2002, a man arrested on drug charges was shot to death in an AFI holding cell. The alleged murderer was a former member of the army's special forces and worked as a *madrina* for AFI agents. Several months later, *madrinas* killed a woman when they accompanied AFI agents on an arrest in Sinaloa in January 2003. They had broken into the home of a suspected drug criminal in order to arrest him—without a warrant—and in the firefight that ensued his sister was killed and his mother injured. It has also been alleged that AFI agents in Nuevo Laredo were involved in a number of disappearances.

The context in which drug law enforcement occurs allows it to be used as a weapon by local political bosses against opponents. Human rights organizations have documented that the criminal justice system is "used as a means of political control by corrupt local officials in drug producing areas. Peasants who grow marijuana and other banned crops are at the mercy of officials who engage in selective enforcement of drug laws and raid and arrest anyone who engages in dissent."

Although lower than in previous years, drug-related arrests in Mexico since 1995 have hovered at around 10,000 a year, and about 90 percent of those accused of drug crimes are found guilty. Those imprisoned tend to come from the poorest sectors of society. In 2001, about three-fourths of the approximately 20,000 people convicted on federal charges (including more than 9,000 for drug crimes) had only an elementary or middle-school education and more than half were farmers or day laborers. According to the CNDH [National Human Rights Commission], nearly one-third of the indigenous prisoners in Mexico in 2001 were in prison for federal crimes, overwhelmingly drug related. Mexico's indigenous population is the poorest, most marginalized, and most vulnerable to abuses by drug traffickers, the police and military, and the justice system. "The majority of these indigenous prisoners are used by organized crime to transport drugs," stated a CNDH official. "Faced with hunger, poor quality lands, without resources to cultivate, and left out of development efforts, indigenous people accept or are forced to transport drugs. They have to find some way to survive."

Although the Fox administration has made an effort to target more high-level traffickers, the vast majority of people imprisoned on drug charges continue to be from the lowest rungs of the drug trade. Of the nearly 19,000 people arrested for drug crimes between December 2000 and April 2003, 98 percent were growers or low-level dealers.

Between 1996 and 2000, soldiers taking part in antidrug operations were implicated in at least fourteen extrajudicial executions.

Human Rights Abuses

The Mexican military has committed a range of human rights violations in the context of antidrug efforts, as soldiers patrol mountain regions and border areas to eradicate and intercept illegal drugs. Human rights organizations have documented scores of cases in recent years, including illegal arrests, secret and prolonged detention, torture, rape, extrajudicial execution, and fabrication of evidence. The military often attempts to refute these allegations through outright denials or false arrest and medical reports. In Fox's first six months in office, the CNDH received eighty complaints by civilians against military personnel, fifty-four of them related to antidrug operations, as well as twenty-six complaints by members of the military against their superiors.

Only agents of the AFI are authorized to carry out arrest warrants for drug crimes, but soldiers can make arrests if they catch someone in the act. In the first six months of 2003, the military arrested 914 alleged drug criminals, nearly one-third of all drug-related arrests during that period. This is a substantial share for an institution that is not legally empowered to conduct criminal investigations and that can carry out arrests only in what should be considered exceptional situations (i.e., without a warrant).

Soldiers have taken advantage of the in flagrante provision to arrest people they consider suspicious but who have not been caught in the act of a crime. After being arrested, detainees have been held for a prolonged time in military custody while evidence is gathered, often through the use of coercion or torture to elicit a confession. Once this evidence has been obtained, the military transfers the detainees to the custody of the civilian authorities.

Soldiers have also committed extrajudicial executions. Between 1996 and 2000, soldiers taking part in antidrug operations were implicated in at least fourteen extrajudicial executions. In some of the cases, the victims died as a result of torture. In others, they were shot by soldiers on drug patrol in rural communities and left to bleed to death. The military often denied its involvement or attempted to justify the executions by claiming that the victims were drug traffickers.

Civilian authorities have reinforced, and even encouraged, the army's abusive actions by validating evidence gathered through torture and by ignoring clear signs of human rights violations and improper procedure. This has occurred even in cases where their own forensic doctors detected torture. The CNDH documented one such case from May 1996 in which a man was illegally detained by soldiers in Guadalajara, taken to a military base, interrogated about drug trafficking, and tortured until he lost consciousness. Four days after his arrest, soldiers took him to the police, claiming they had just arrested him in the act of a crime. Although a government physician certified evidence of torture, which should have invalidated the confession that was the basis of the charges against him, civilian authorities charged him with drug crimes. Eight similar cases from Guadalajara during the same period were documented by the CNDH, with civilian authorities charging suspected criminals on the basis of confessions extracted by soldiers through the use of torture.

The military often provides backup for civilian police, and sometimes police even ask soldiers to carry out tasks. In one case from February 2002, AFI agents asked the Mexican military to locate a particular criminal defense attorney who was implicated in a drug case and to bring him in for questioning. Military police organized an operation to detain him after he made a prison visit to one of his clients. As the target was driving away from the prison, a group of nonuniformed soldiers attempted to stop his vehicle. When he did not heed their orders they opened fire on the car, forcing it off the road and killing one of the passengers inside. The soldiers detained the lawyer (without a warrant) and brought him to the civilian authorities for questioning, leaving his companion to bleed to death.

Most [human rights abuse] cases are not investigated; those investigated are rarely prosecuted.

Political Repression

Sending the army into rural regions for counterdrug operations can also serve as cover for counterinsurgency efforts. Since the 1990s, the Mexican army has maintained a large presence in Guerrero, a region known for poverty, illicit crop cultivation, and opposition movements, both peaceful and armed. Civil society organizations active in regions affected by drug trafficking have long suspected that they were subjects of military surveillance. Organizations in Chihuahua had their suspicions confirmed by a Defense Ministry document outlining a plan for establishing antidrug working groups that

> will adopt the measures necessary to obtain information on the existence of armed groups, subversive activities, unjustifiable presence of foreigners, organizations, proselytizing by priests or leaders of religious sects, ecological groups, political propaganda, [and] the presence and activities of bands or gangs of criminals.

Soldiers have conducted counterdrug sweeps that target local activists and intimidate communities where they suspect insurgent activities. According to Human Rights Watch,

> The counterinsurgency mindset appears to be reproduced in the army's approach to the drug war, as officers rely on . . . their perceived political allies for information about who to target in their operations. In this way, *caciques*—or political bosses—are able to bring the firepower of the army to bear upon their political opponents by denouncing them as guerrillas or drug traffickers.

Illustrative of this danger is the case of environmental activists Rodolfo Montiel and Teodoro Cabrera. Their campaign against logging angered local *caciques*, who then denounced them as drug traffickers to regional military commanders. The men were illegally arrested by soldiers who tortured them into confessing to trumped-up drug and gun charges. Both men were convicted; Amnesty International declared them prisoners of conscience. Despite that, their case is listed as one of the "important convictions"—along with that of Colima cartel kingpin Adán Amezcua Contreras—in a document highlighting the Zedillo administration's major antidrug accomplishments.

Impunity for human rights violations committed by the military is a serious problem. Most cases are not investigated; those investigated are rarely prosecuted; and the few convictions for human rights abuse that have been reached came after years of national and international pressure. The military justice system has jurisdiction over cases in which military personnel are blamed for abuses against civilians. Military courts are not transparent or accountable to civilian authorities or victims, and military justice officials are legally prohibited from making documents from judicial proceedings public. Even soldiers seconded to police forces like the PFP

[Federal Preventive Police] remain under military jurisdiction if they commit human rights violations against civilians while on police duty.

The Role of the United States

Under a U.S. law known as the Leahy Amendment, no member or unit of a foreign security force that is credibly alleged to have committed a human rights violation may receive U.S. training. Furthermore, no unit of a foreign security force can receive equipment or other assistance if any of its members is suspected of human rights abuse, unless the government is taking steps toward bringing that person to justice.

U.S. embassy officials in Mexico in charge of human rights and drug control programs state that they vet all proposed police and military trainees for alleged involvement in human rights violation. However, human rights groups monitoring Leahy Amendment implementation in Mexico say it is not clear that the embassy is doing adequate human rights vetting of the police personnel and units that are receiving U.S. assistance. The embassy database that keeps track of human rights violations is seriously incomplete. One human rights organization submitted information to the embassy on more than sixty well-documented cases of human rights abuse by the Mexican military, yet only a few had been registered in the database. Embassy officials reported that they had never asked the military for information about judicial actions against soldiers implicated in abuse. Given this lax oversight, and considering the thousands of soldiers and police that have been trained or have benefited from U.S. assistance, it is possible that some abusive agents received U.S. training or other assistance.

The United States has provided training to members of the Mexican military who have gone on to commit human rights violations. In December 1997, a group of heavily armed Mexican special forces soldiers kidnapped twenty young men in Ocotlán, Jalisco, brutally torturing them and killing one. Six of the implicated officers had received U.S. training as part of the GAFE [Air-Mobile Special Forces Group] training program.

Torture

U.S. officials have also sought to use evidence that was obtained through torture. In one case reported by the *New York Times*, an agent from the Bureau of Alcohol, Tobacco, and Firearms (ATF) interrogated Alejandro Hodoyan Palacios, a Tijuana cartel enforcer suspected of murdering a Mexican antidrug prosecutor. Hodoyan had been arrested by the Mexican military and subjected to torture during his incommunicado detention; when the ATF agent met with Hodoyan, the latter was blindfolded and shackled to a bed in a military barracks. The DEA also had a chance to debrief the suspect and "eagerly accepted the offer as a rare chance to cooperate with the Mexican military and improve their relations" with drug czar Gutiérrez Rebollo. The U.S. government indicted Hodoyan for drug crimes, even though the evidence against him had been "gathered with methods that would not be permitted under American law." U.S. prosecutors found themselves in the position of defending the quality of Mexico's evidence.

The U.S. government has even hailed some abusive investigations as evidence of Mexico's commitment to the war on drugs. For example, in October 2002, military authorities held hundreds of soldiers incommunicado to investigate reports that they were protecting drug traffickers. Military police and prosecutors, aided by army special forces groups, threatened, beat, and tortured soldiers in order to obtain information and confessions. The Mexican government's National Human Rights Commission documented that several soldiers bore physical evidence of torture such as bruised stomachs, backs, and testicles. Thirteen soldiers were eventually charged with drug crimes, and the entire battalion was disbanded. The State

Department pointed to the prosecutions as a success in the war on drugs, citing the effort as an example of how "Mexican leaders worked energetically to detect and punish corruption among law enforcement officials and military personnel." But the use of torture raises questions about the validity of the charges.

U.S. agents have themselves been involved in extrajudicial action on Mexican territory. In 1990, the DEA organized a secret operation to apprehend a Mexican citizen allegedly involved in the [DEA agent Enrique] Camarena murder. Using a tactic known as "irregular rendition," DEA agents, frustrated by corruption and the lack of cooperation from their Mexican counterparts, hired a man to kidnap Humberto Álvarez Machain and bring him to the United States for prosecution. This incident reinforced the impression that law enforcement agents may flout the law if their illegal actions ultimately result in the arrest and prosecution of suspected traffickers. It also aggravated tensions in the bilateral relationship, as Mexico had very real grievances about violations of its sovereignty.

In a more recent case, agents at the U.S. Bureau of Immigration and Customs Enforcement (ICE) kept a Juárez cartel hit man as a paid informant despite knowing of his participation in the murders of at least twelve suspected drug traffickers. This man's activities, and ICE's knowledge of them, came to light after he organized an assassination attempt against two DEA agents living in Juárez in January 2004. Perhaps to deflect attention from himself, the informant helped U.S. agents capture a prominent Juárez cartel member, which in turn led to the discovery of a clandestine graveyard in the backyard of a former Chihuahua state police officer's home where the bodies of the twelve suspected drug traffickers were buried.

According to U.S. and Mexican officials, one of the victims had been killed several months earlier by the informant, whose ICE handlers had been notified ahead of time and listened in on an open cellphone line as he tortured and murdered the man; the agency later altered an internal memorandum in an effort to cover up the informant's role in the killing. By continuing its relationship with the informant despite knowledge of his responsibility for torture and murder, U.S. officials signaled that such illegal and unethical practices were an acceptable price to pay for information about drug trafficking.

Drug Cartels Threaten the Rule of Law in Mexico

Larry Birns and Alex Sánchez

Larry Birns is the director of the Council on Hemispheric Affairs (COHA), a not-for-profit organization that promotes a better relationship between the United States and Latin America. Alex Sánchez is a research fellow at COHA.

In Mexico, President Felipe Calderon may be the constitutionally-elected leader of the nation, but in reality, drug cartels and warlords exercise *de facto* authority over much of the area. During President [George W.] Bush's two-day stopover in Mexico as part of his recent [March 13–14, 2007] Latin American tour, he wasted no time in praising the accomplishments of the Calderon administration in combating drug trafficking. At a joint press conference with the Mexican leader in Merida (March 14), Bush said that: "President Calderon is taking a tough stand against organized crime and drugs, and I appreciate that." He went on to say that: "I recognize the United States has a responsibility in the fight against drugs. And one major responsibility is to encourage people to use less drugs. When there is demand, there is supply."

Now that Calderon is firmly installed as president of Mexico, . . . the new leader has shown, at least on the surface, that he is ready to tackle his country's major problems: organized crime and gross impunity. Drug trafficking overwhelmingly is the prevailing social malady throughout the country, particularly along the border with the U.S. In spite of lengthy declarations by government officials in Mexico City and Washington, and their insistence that important battles are being won against drug trafficking, criminal organizations like the

Larry Birns and Alex Sánchez, "The Government and the Drug Lords: Who Rules Mexico?," *Council on Hemispheric Affairs*, April 10, 2007. Reproduced by permission.

Tijuana cartel continue to thrive, ruling over whole sections of the Mexican countryside like sectoral feudal lords. . . .

Drug Trafficking

The governor of the state of Nuevo Leon (bordering the U.S.), Natividad Gonzalez Paras has declared that "unfortunately, the problem has escalated significantly in the past six to seven years. It is a national problem affecting most of the country's states. It is a dispute between cartels or organizations to control locations, cities and routes." This observation may in fact understate the current situation. The International Narcotics Control Board (INCB) in Vienna has issued a report, stating that Mexican drug trafficking organizations and the criminal groups which control most of the organized drug traffic in the United States, particularly cocaine, marijuana, methamphetamines and heroin have not been giving stellar performances. In 2004, U.S. authorities seized approximately 580 tons of cannabis coming from Mexico, which provides some indication of the magnitude of the drugs currently produced and trafficked in Mexico. According to the Mexican daily *La Voz de la Frontera*, the INCB's annual report states that Mexico produced over 10,000 tons of marijuana in 2005, in contrast to the 4,500 tons produced in the United States, making the former the region's largest supplier of marijuana. Other reports indicate that the combined worth of the marijuana and cocaine being transported from Mexico into the U.S. each year has reached an estimated $50 billion. Major crossing points for these drugs are to be found in Arizona, California and Texas.

Violence between rival cartels continues to be a daily occurrence.

Of the huge volume of different categories of drugs smuggled across the border into the U.S. market, only a small amount are being seized by Mexican authorities. According to a December 20, 2006 article in the Mexican newspaper *El Diario*, figures provided by the Mexican Defense Secretariat show that in 2006, Mexican military units had seized a paltry 13 kg of marijuana, no cocaine, and seven firearms, [and] only arrested a total of 10 suspects on drug-related crimes in the border state of Nuevo Leon. The article goes on to explain that the amount of seized marijuana peaked in 2001 with 3,912 tons, and since then has been in steady decline. In 2002 and 2003, authorities confiscated 1,106 tons and 1,616 tons of marijuana, respectively, only to see it plummet to 849 kg in 2004, and to 310 kg in 2006. Later in 2006, the number further fell to 13 kg. In terms of cocaine confiscations, Mexican military personnel responsible for maintaining four permanent checkpoints along the principal access highways to Ciudad Juarez, had failed to confiscate even one gram of cocaine by the time the *El Diario* article had appeared; this was in contrast to 2001, when they had seized 18.9 kg of cocaine. Given these graphic statistics of underperformance, it is not hard to explain why the flow of narcotics through states like Nuevo Leon has been declining. Violence between rival cartels continues to be a daily occurrence in the affected areas. It is therefore all but incomprehensible why anti-drug authorities repeatedly claim interdictions of drug flow when in fact they are actually shrugging off their responsibilities by frequently closing their eyes to the massive drug shipments taking place. The result is a hugely damaging co-conspiracy between Bush and Calderon, with the anti-drug establishment and the criminal law system in both countries being fueled by the oceans of public funds. It now has become a fight for one's weekly salary and one's share of the immense amount of corruption that has been available by the debilitating flood of illicit payments buying public officials. The drug war goes on in spite of its relatively rare and spotty successes, because too much is at stake to end it. The moral here being: pretense pays.

Some criminal organizations like the Sinaloa drug cartel have even transported some of their infrastructure to the U.S., namely to the Texan city of Laredo. Here, Texas police officers are finding a growing number of safe houses being utilized by the cartel as logistical staging points to organize drug shipments and initiate armed attacks on the American side of the border. In addition, as explained in a March 2006 *Dallas Morning News* article, there is another reason for the movement of drug cartel operations north of the border. According to the article, there is a "soft justice" in the U.S. in comparison to Mexico: cartel operatives in the Laredo-Nuevo Laredo area are well-aware of the fact that if they are apprehended north of the Texas-Mexico border, they likely will go to jail and be able to fight extradition to Mexico by means of their expensive U.S. legal teams. On the other hand, if they are detained south of the border, they are more likely to be murdered in their jail cells by members of rival cartels, by Nuevo Laredo's corrupt law enforcement officials, or by Tamaulitas' state police.

Government Victories

There have been a number of important victories by Mexican authorities against drug trafficking, including seizures of illicit narcotics and the capture of high level drug lords. These accomplishments are relatively few in number and staccato in nature, with a long hiatus often following some stunning benchmark in the antidrug war. Therefore, it remains far from certain if the new Mexican government has managed to make a dent in drug-related crimes across the country. The most important anti-crime operation in recent months has been, according to Ciudad Victoria's *El Diario*, the Mexican army's seizure in late March of a 7.5 ton shipment of marijuana hidden in a trailer carrying avocadoes being shipped from Uruapan, Michoacan, apparently intended for export to the U.S. market. Meanwhile, in Coahuila, the Mexican police and army have recommended setting up random checkpoints in La Laguna. Such an operation would include regular helicopter sur-veillance of rural areas around Lerdo. As a result of operations already initiated, 22 people have been detained for drug pos-session. Another success was the January 16 [2007] arrest of drug kingpin Pedro Diaz Parada, the head of the "Diaz Parada" cartel that operates in southern Mexico. Diaz Parada is known to have shot Judge Pedro Villafuerte 33 times, (once for each year of prison to which he had been sentenced by Villafuerte).

Calderon's Winter Offensives

Anti-drug operations under Mexican President Felipe Cal-deron widened as a result of his decision to dispatch more federal police officers to the U.S.-Mexican border in order to curb the violence and slash the volume of drug trafficking. As many as 17,000 troops have been deployed to areas that previ-ously resembled the lawless regions of Somalia, with little con-trol being exercised by the central government. The large numbers indicate the magnitude of the deployment that Cal-deron has been willing to carry out as part of his nationwide plans: he has sent as many as 3,000 security personnel to Baja California, particularly to the border city of Tijuana. In addi-tion, he has sent 6,300 troops and federal police to the state of Guerrero and 9,054 personnel to Sierra Madre. This region is of particular structural importance as it is one of the centers of the expansion of drug trafficking, particularly marijuana, and includes part of the states of Chihuahua, Durango and Si-naloa. Other reports mention that Calderon has assigned 7,000 officials to the state of Michoacan. These offensives have come with mixed but usually bloody results. The bottom line here is that Calderon will find it both expensive and distortive to the country's economy to dispatch large numbers of security per-sonnel to only one of the country's theaters. Past experiences have been to launch showcase anti-drug offensives but see them settle down in short order.

Victories and Defeats

Last January [2006], Mexican authorities reported that they had detained 80 suspects on drug traffic-related charges, as well as seizing hundreds of kilograms of marijuana, in major operations carried out in Michoacan. The most important detention in the latest offensives was that of a Gulf cartel leader, Jeremias Ramirez Garcia, also known as *Carne Seca* (dry meat). He is believed to be a member of the Zetas, former elite Mexican commandos that turned corrupt and who now have been hired by the drug cartels as hitmen. Another victory is the capture of Pedro Diaz Parada, which has also been attributed to Calderon's strategies. Overall, the government is claiming as victories the destruction of 1,500 hectares of illicit crops, like marijuana, as well as the seizure of 32 tons of the substance, along with 2.2 tons of cocaine.

There have been a growing number of assassinations, which most likely can be attributed to the drug cartels "punishing" the government.

For these professed achievements, much praise has been accorded to Calderon by a White House that wants to believe in the success of the anti-drug war. A January 27 editorial in the *Chicago Tribune* amply saluted the Mexican leader, observing how "in the long, hard fight against an intractable problem, Calderon has given notice that he means business" and that he is "serious about shutting down the drug cartels and their escalating lawlessness." However, as hailed as such praise was and, meant to be, it was little better than a Potemkin Village similar to the language used to praise his predecessor, Vicente Fox, soon after he took office and declared a war on drugs, which soon evaporated.

At the time, American government officials and the media praised Fox for his antidrug measures, but today the former president is cryptically portrayed as not having done nearly enough to cope with drugs. A June 16, 2005 *Washington Post* article by Mary Jordan and Kevin Sullivan . . . reported how Washington continually had praised Fox's efforts, noting that he had jailed more top cartel leaders than any Mexican president in history. However, the article concludes on perhaps a less celebratory if more accurate note by noting the conclusions of Mexican academic Jorge Chabat, whose words can be applied to both Fox and now Calderon's efforts to combat aspects of the Mexican drug problem. Chabat explains that: "the good news is that there are more *capos* [head of a branch of a syndicate] in jail; the bad news is that it doesn't change anything. There's no change in the amount of drugs available in the street, and you have more violence. The logical question is, 'What are we doing this for?'"

A state of lawlessness continues to prevail throughout Mexico.

Corruption + Deaths

For whatever government victories may have been achieved against organized crime and their drug cartels, there also has been plenty of retaliatory action against government officials and security forces. In the past several months there have been a growing number of assassinations, which most likely can be attributed to the drug cartels "punishing" the government. These acts have included the murder of Vidal Ivan Barraza Lujan, son of Vidal Barraza (commander of the Special Prosecutor's Office for the Investigation of Homicides against Women), who was gunned-down as he traveled in Chihuahua. Another victim of vengeance was Abraham Eduardo Farias Martinez, a state law enforcement commander and SWAT leader, who was murdered on February 28 [2007] as he headed to an anti-drug meeting. He was shot several times in the head by a hired assassin. Commander Farias Martinez's murder is the eighth homicide of an agent this year, and the 17th registered in Nuevo Leon since the beginning of 2007.

On February 19 [2007], there was an attempt to assassinate Horacio Garza, a federal deputy from the Partido Revolucionario Institucional in Nuevo Laredo, and a former mayor of that town. Garza's driver was killed and Garza himself is in intensive care after their car was riddled by machine gun fire as it traveled to the airport. President Calderon has acknowledged that even he and his family have received death threats as a result of his publicized anti-drug trafficking offensive.

Such incidents make one wonder if the new president and his statement of avowed aggressive policing and beefing up the number of Mexican troops along the border, are making any significant headway. Perhaps the most disturbing aspect of the increasingly violent domestic violence now being recorded are the deaths of SWAT leader Martinez as well as Alejandro Dominguez. In 2005, Dominguez had been appointed the new police chief in the border city of Nuevo Laredo, mostly because he was the only person brave enough to volunteer to assume such a position. He was murdered only hours after being sworn in, by henchmen who riddled him with automatic fire. The grim fates of the aforementioned Martinez and Dominguez should fix the idea that state of lowlessness continues to prevail throughout Mexico, in spite of declarations to the contrary, and not even those wearing badges are especially safe.

Last year [2006], 2,000 people were murdered as a result of drug-related crimes. Between 2000 and 2006, there were around 9,000 fatal casualties directly or indirectly resulting from drug trafficking, according to an Inter-Press Service report.

Drug cartels also have become bolder in selecting their assassination targets and methods of execution. Long gone are the days when a killing was done in the middle of the night,

Hollywood style, with the victim's body promptly buried in a make-shift grave in the woods. This was done in order to get rid of the evidence and avoid any potential police investigation. Today, it is carried out much more casually; a murder victim may simply be thrown in the waters of the Rio Grande, or left to decompose in the middle of a field. Killings often occur in daytime, often by way of drive-by shootings or by attacks in popular places like malls or restaurants. The weapons used by criminals also have changed. They no longer are simply revolvers but have swelled to machine guns, grenades and even barrels of acid (used both for torture and a body's disposal). Beheadings also have become a popular method of execution. In addition, it does not help to attempt to bring the rule of law to a country where corruption and fear of cartels have become an endemic problem within the nation's security forces.

The *vox populi* [general public] believe that many police officers, government officials, and judges are on the bankroll of the different cartels, thus hindering presidential initiatives to put drug criminals behind bars. Even if a police officer does not work for the cartel but is "clean," he (or she) may be too afraid to act against them out of fear of a bloody reprisal. Those few brave souls that do stand up to fight the criminal gangs, like Dominguez in Nuevo Laredo, usually do not survive for long.

More Extradition to the U.S.

The extradition of Mexican drug lords and other top cartel bosses to the U.S. is becoming more and more popular among American policymakers because they distrust the ability of the Mexican criminal law system to effectively try suspects and, if found guilty, to have them sent off to the country's notoriously porous penitentiary system, where the drug lords will "escape" in a scripted manner or remain incarcerated only to see the cut in communications between them and their home cartels. An example of this was the case of Osiel Cardenas, who for four years ran his Gulf cartel from behind the bars of a maximum-security prison in Mexico. There are reports that, while in prison, he even sponsored a "Day of the Children" party in the border town of Reynosa, complete with truck-loads of toys and notes that read that they were a compliment of "jailbird Cardenas." It was only when Cardenas, along with other drug kingpins, [was] handed to U.S. authorities that their control over their organizations began to unravel.

Rampant corruption and drug-related violence discourage foreign investment and prevent development.

Extradition is a complicated process that involves sovereignty and legal issues, and which comes with mixed blessings and curses. One profound example of a downside is that extradition effectively undermines the Mexican legal and penitentiary system. Essentially, individuals who commit crimes on Mexican soil and are captured by Mexican authorities, are being handed over to the justice system of another country because their own system is not viewed as effective and is vulnerable to threats and intimidation.

Calderon is likely to continue Mexico's recent policy of supporting extradition to the U.S., which will certainly earn him praise and approval from Washington policymakers, even if Washington's war against drugs deserves anything less than a shrug. It was under the recently inaugurated Calderon presidency that Osiel Cardenas, along with three other drug kingpins and eleven other lesser criminals were extradited north of the border. U.S. Ambassador to Mexico, Antonio O. Garza, has described the extradition as a "monumental moment in our two nations' battle with the vicious drug traffickers and criminals who threaten our very way of life."

Anti-Drug Failures

Drug trafficking is Mexico's cancer, bringing the population an indescribable number of problems, while it is barely being noticed back in the U.S. The issue is not simply the thousands of deaths in drug-related incidents every year, but also the government's inability to control the drug cartels. This situation creates a profound sense of fatalism and disillusionment over the ability of elected officials and the security forces to effectively cope with crime and to honestly bring law and order to the community. Furthermore, rampant corruption and drug-related violence discourage foreign investment and prevent development, two issues that Mexico needs to resolve.

Even if Mexican authorities are able to occasionally apprehend major drug kingpins, who are later extradited to U.S. prisons, this situation would only leave a power vacuum within the cartel in which ten different drug "lieutenants" would try to fill. Ultimately, it is a near certainty that this would trigger intra-gang violence as drug lieutenants launch internecine combat in a personal quest for power, which in the process will certainly claim many innocent civilian lives. Just this past March 29–30 [2007], gunmen killed two Mexican police officers and six civilians in less than 48 hours in the city of Monterrey in Nuevo Leon. Apparently the deaths came as a result of inter-gang warfare over turf between the Sinaloa and the Gulf cartels. Over 200 rounds were shot at a group of six men, killing three and injuring others, who apparently had no connection to the drug trade and were simply standing outside the wrong house at the wrong time.

The current plan to combat drug trafficking in Mexico is simply not working. Unfortunately, no other viable alternative solution exists with the exception of the further deployment of the Mexican army to lawless regions and the subsequent extradition of drug criminals to the U.S. While some praise can be given to Fox and Calderon for wholeheartedly taking measures to curb drug trafficking and violence in the nation, in reality it has been more a matter of appearance than a hard and lasting fact. In this respect, Calderon is already on the same path that Fox eventually took: much thunder but little lightening.

Drug-Related Corruption Threatens the Rule of Law in Guatemala

Frank Smyth

Frank Smyth is a freelance journalist.

The alert went out across the state [of Texas] this past July [2005]. A McAllen-based FBI [Federal Bureau of Investigation] analyst wrote a classified report that the Department of Homeland Security sent to U.S. Border Patrol agents throughout Texas. About 30 suspects who were once part of an elite unit of the Guatemalan special forces were training drug traffickers in paramilitary tactics just over the border from McAllen. The unit, called the *Kaibiles* after the Mayan prince Kaibil Balam, is one of the most fearsome military forces in Latin America, blamed for many of the massacres that occurred in Guatemala during its 36-year civil war. By September, Mexican authorities announced that they had arrested seven Guatemalan Kaibiles, including four "deserters" who were still listed by the Guatemalan Army as being on active duty.

The Kaibiles and La Cofradia

Mexican authorities say the Kaibiles were meant to augment Las Zetas, a drug gang of soldiers-turned-hitmen drawn from Mexico's own special forces. It's logical that the Zetas would turn to their Guatemalan counterparts. In addition to being a neighbor, "Guatemala is the preferred transit point in Central America for onward shipment of cocaine to United States," the State Department has consistently reported to Congress since 1999. In early November [2005] anti-drug authorities at

Frank Smyth, "The Untouchable Narco-State," *Texas Observer*, November 18, 2005. Reproduced by permission.

the U.S. Embassy in Guatemala told the Associated Press that 75 percent of the cocaine that reaches American soil passes through the Central American nation.

More importantly, perhaps, the dominant institution in the country—the military—is linked to this illicit trade. Over the past two decades, the U.S. Drug Enforcement Administration (DEA) has quietly accused Guatemalan military officers of all ranks in every branch of service of trafficking drugs to the United States, according to government documents obtained by *The Texas Observer*. More recently, the Bush administration has alleged that two retired Guatemalan Army generals, at the top of the country's military hierarchy, are involved in drug trafficking and has revoked their U.S. visas based on these allegations.

There is enough evidence implicating the Guatemalan military in illegal activities that the Bush administration no longer gives U.S. military aid.

The retired generals, Manuel Antonio Callejas y Callejas and Francisco Ortega Menaldo, are Guatemala's former top two intelligence chiefs. They are also among the founders of an elite, shadowy club within Guatemala's intelligence command that calls itself "*la cofradia*" or "the brotherhood," according to U.S. intelligence reports. The U.S. reports, recently de-classified, credit *la cofradia* with "engineering" tactics that roundly defeated Guatemala's Marxist guerrillas. A U.N. [United Nations] Truth Commission later found the same tactics included "acts of genocide" for driving out or massacring the populations of no less than 440 Mayan villages.

Guatemala's military intelligence commands developed a code of silence during these bloody operations, which is one reason why no officer was ever prosecuted for any Cold War–era human rights abuses. Since then, the same intelligence commands have turned their clandestine structures to organized crimes, according to DEA and other U.S. intelligence reports, from importing stolen U.S. cars to running drugs to the United States. Yet not one officer has ever been prosecuted for any international crime in either Guatemala or the United States.

A Weak Government

There is enough evidence implicating the Guatemalan military in illegal activities that the Bush administration no longer gives U.S. military aid, including officer training. The cited offenses include "a recent resurgence of abuses believed to be orchestrated by ex-military and current military officials; and allegations of corruption and narcotics trafficking by ex-military officers," according to the State Department's 2004 report on Foreign Military Training.

While some in the Bush administration and Congress want to restart foreign military training, others are concerned about the inability of the Guatemalan government to rein in its military. "The reason that elements of the army are involved so deeply in this illicit operation is that the government simply does not have the power to stop them," said Texas Republican Congressman Michael McCaul, who sits on the Western Hemisphere Subcommittee of the Committee on International Relations and is the Chairman of the Department of Homeland Security Subcommittee on Investigations.

> *Guatemala has long been sluggish in efforts to take legal action against its military officers for human rights violations.*

Guatemala is hardly the first military tainted by drugs; senior intelligence and law enforcement officer in many Latin American nations have been found colluding with organized crime. But what distinguishes Guatemala from most other nations is that some of its military suspects are accused not only of protecting large criminal syndicates but of being the ringleaders behind them. The Bush administration has recently credited both Colombia and Mexico with making unprecedented strides in both prosecuting their own drug suspects and extraditing others to the United States. But Guatemala, alone in this hemisphere, has failed to either prosecute or extradite any of its own alleged drug kingpins for at least 10 years.

For decades, successive U.S. administrations have tried and failed to train effective Guatemalan police, while saying little or nothing about the known criminal activities of the Guatemalan military. That finally came to an end in the past three years under Republican Rep. Cass Ballenger, a staunch conservative from North Carolina, who served as chairman of the Western Hemisphere Subcommittee.

"Clearly, the Guatemalan government has not taken every step needed to investigate, arrest, and bring drug kingpins to justice," said then-Chairman Ballenger in 2003 before he retired. Echoing his predecessor, the new Chairman, Indiana Republican Rep. Dan Burton, commented through a spokesman that he wants to see the same alleged ringleaders finally brought "to full accountability."

Until that happens, drugs from Guatemala and the attendant violence will continue to spill over the Texas border.

No Accountability

Guatemala has long been sluggish in efforts to take legal action against its military officers for human rights violations. That impunity has since spread to organized criminal acts as well. The turning point came in 1994, when Guatemala's extraditions of its drug suspects came to a dead stop over a case involving an active duty army officer. The case highlights both the terrible price for those who seek justice in Guatemala and the timidity of the United States in demanding accountability.

A military intelligence officer back in the early 1980s, Lt. Col. Carlos Ochoa briefly trained at the U.S. Army Command and General Staff College in 1988. Two years later, the DEA accused him of smuggling drugs to locations including Florida, where DEA special agents seized a small plane with half a metric ton of cocaine, allegedly sent by the colonel.

State Department attorneys worked for more than three years to keep Guatemala's military tribunals from dismissing the charges, and finally brought Ochoa's extradition case all the way to Guatemala's highest civilian court. The nation's chief justice, Epaminondas González Dubón, was already well respected for his integrity. On March 23, 1994, Guatemala's Constitutional Court, led by González Dubón, quietly ruled in a closed session (which is common in Guatemala) four-to-three in favor of extraditing Ochoa.

Nine days later, on April 1, gunmen shot and killed González Dubón behind the wheel of his own car in the capital, near his middle-class home, in front of his wife and youngest son. On April 12, the same Constitutional Court, with a new chief justice, quietly ruled seven-to-one not to extradite Ochoa. The surviving judges used the same line in the official Constitutional Court register—changing the verdict and date, but not the original case number—to literally copy over the original ruling, as was only reported years later by the Costa Rican daily, *La Nación*.

U.S. Complicity

The Clinton administration never said one word in protest. The U.S. ambassador in Guatemala City at the time, Marilyn McAfee, by her own admission had other concerns, including ongoing peace talks with the Guatemalan military. "I am concerned over the potential decline in our relationship with the military," she wrote to her superiors only months before the assassination. "The bottom line is we must carefully consider each of our actions toward the Guatemalan military, not only for how it plays in Washington, but for how it impacts here."

Four years after the murder, the [President Bill] Clinton administration finally admitted in a few lines buried in a thick report to Congress: "The Chief Justice of the Constitutional Court had approved (the) extradition for the 1991 charges just before he was assassinated. The reconstituted court soon thereafter voted to deny the extradition."

Ochoa may not have been working alone. "In addition to his narcotics trafficking activities, Ochoa was involved in bringing stolen cars from the U.S. to Guatemala," reads a "SE-CRET" U.S. intelligence report obtained by U.S. lawyer Jennifer Harbury. "Another military officer involved with Ochoa in narcotics trafficking is Colonel Julio Roberto Alpírez de Leon."

Alpírez, who briefly trained at the U.S. School of the Americas in 1970, served "in special intelligence operations," according to a U.S. Defense Intelligence Agency (DIA) report. A White House Oversight Board investigation later implicated him in the torture and murder of a Marxist guerrilla leader who was married to the Harvard-trained lawyer Harbury, and in the torture and mysterious decapitation of an American hotelier named Michael Devine. Col. Alpírez, since retired, has denied any wrongdoing and he was never charged with any crime.

But Ochoa, his former subordinate, is in jail today. Ochoa was arrested—again—for local cocaine dealing in Guatemala City, where crack smoking and violent crimes, especially rape, have become alarmingly common. Ochoa was later sentenced to 14 years in prison, and he remains the most important drug criminal ever convicted in Guatemala to date.

Until now, the DEA had never publicly recognized the bravery of Judge González Dubón, who died defending DEA evidence. "The judge deserves to be remembered and honored for trying to help establish democracy in Guatemala," said

DEA senior special agent William Glaspy in an exclusive interview. Since the murder, the DEA has been all but impotent in Guatemala.

A History of Impunity

The impunity that shields Guatemalan military officers from justice for criminal offenses started during the Cold War. "There is a long history of impunity in Guatemala," noted Congressman William Delahunt, a Democrat from Massachusetts, who is also a member of the Western Hemisphere Subcommittee. "The United States has contributed to it in a very unsavory way dating back to 1954, and also in the 1980s," he added, referring to a CIA [Central Intelligence Agency] backed coup d'état in 1954, which overturned a democratically elected president and brought the Guatemalan military to power, and to the [President Ronald] Reagan administration's covert backing of the Guatemalan military at a time when bloodshed against Guatemalan civilians was peaking.

It was also during this Cold War–era carnage that the army's *la cofradía* came into its own.

"The mere mention of the word '*cofradía*' inside the institution conjures up the idea of the 'intelligence club,' the term '*cofradía*' being the name given to the powerful organizations of village-church elders that exist today in the Indian highlands of Guatemala," reads a once-classified 1991 U.S. Defense Intelligence Agency cable. "Many of the 'best and the brightest' of the officers of the Guatemalan Army were brought into intelligence work and into tactical operations planning," it continues. Like all documents not otherwise attributed in this report, the cable was obtained by the non-profit National Security Archives in Washington, D.C.

According to the 1991 cable, "well-known members of this unofficial *cofradía* include" then army colonels "Manuel Antonio Callejas y Callejas" and "Ortega Menaldo." (Each officer had briefly trained at the U.S. School of the Americas, in 1970 and 1976, respectively.)

DEA special agents began detecting Guatemalan military officers running drugs as early as 1986.

The intelligence report goes on: "Under directors of intelligence such as then-Col. Manuel Antonio Callejas y Callejas back in the early 1980s, the intelligence directorate made dramatic gains in its capabilities, so much so that today it must be given the credit for engineering the military decline of the guerrillas from 1982 to the present. But while doing so, the intelligence directorate became an elite 'club' within the officer corps."

Other Guatemalan officers called their approach at the time the practice of "draining the sea to kill the fish," or of attacking civilians suspected of supporting leftist guerrillas instead of the armed combatants themselves. One former Guatemalan Army sergeant, who served in the bloodied province of Quiché, later told this author he learned another expression: "Making the innocent pay for the sins of the guilty."

CIA reports are even more candid, "The commanding officers of the units involved have been instructed to destroy all towns and villages which are cooperating with the guerrilla(s) and eliminate all sources of resistance," reads one 1982 Guatemala City CIA Station report formerly classified "SECRET." The CIA report goes on, "When an Army patrol meets resistance and takes fire from a town or village it is assumed that the entire town is hostile and it is subsequently destroyed." Forensic teams have since exhumed many mass graves. Some unearthed women and infants. More than 200,000 people were killed in Guatemala in what stands as Central America's bloodiest conflict during the Cold War.

The Columbian Connection

The violence left the military firmly in control of Guatemala, and it did not take long for this stability to catch the attention of Colombian drug syndicates. First the Medellín and then the Cali cartels, according to Andean drug experts, began searching for new smuggling routes to the United States after their more traditional routes closed down by the mid-1980s due to greater U.S. radar surveillance over the Caribbean, especially the Bahamas.

"They chose Guatemala because it is near Mexico, which is an obvious entrance point to the U.S., and because the Mexicans have a long-established mafia," explained one Andean law enforcement expert. "It is also a better transit and storage country than El Salvador because it offers more stability and was easier to control."

DEA special agents began detecting Guatemalan military officers running drugs as early as 1986 according to DEA documents obtained through the U.S. Freedom of Information Act. That's when Ortega Menaldo took over from Callejas y Callejas as Guatemala's military intelligence chief. Over the next nine years, according to the same U.S. documents, DEA special agents detected no less than 31 active duty officers running drugs.

"All roads lead to Ortega," a U.S. drug enforcement expert said recently. "Even current active-duty officers may have other ties with retired officers. They have a mentor relationship."

U.S. intelligence reports reveal the strong ties that *cofradía* high-level officers cultivated with many subordinates, who are dubbed "the operators." "This vertical column of intelligence officers, from captains to generals, represents the strongest internal network of loyalties within the institution," reads the 1991 U.S. DIA cable. "Other capable officers were being hand-picked at all levels to serve in key operations and troop command," this U.S. report goes on. "Although not as tight knit as the *cofradía*, the 'operators' all the same developed their own vertical leader-subordinate network of recognition, relationships and loyalties, and are today considered a separate and distinct vertical column of officer loyalties."

Cofradía officers extended their reach even further, according to another U.S. intelligence cable, as the mid-level officer "operators" whom they chose in turn handpicked local civilians to serve as "military commissioners (to be) the 'eyes and ears' of the military" at the grassroots.

The Last Extradition

Few criminal cases better demonstrate the integration between the Guatemalan intelligence commands and drug trafficking than one pursued in 1990 by DEA special agents in the hot, sticky plains of eastern Guatemala, near the nation's Caribbean coast. This 15-year-old case is also the last time that any Guatemalans wanted on drug charges were extradited to the United States. Arnoldo Vargas Estrada, a.k.a. "Archie," was a long-time local "military commissioner," and the elected mayor of the large town of Zacapa. U.S. embassy officials informed (as is still required according to diplomatic protocol between the two nations) Guatemalan military intelligence, then led by Ortega Menaldo, that DEA special agents had the town mayor under surveillance.

Vargas and two other civilian suspects were then arrested in Guatemala with the help of the DEA. Not long after, all three men were extradited to New York, where they were tried and convicted on DEA evidence. But the DEA did nothing back in Guatemala when, shortly after the arrests, the military merely moved the same smuggling operation to a rural area outside town, according to family farmers in a petition delivered to the U.S. Embassy in Guatemala City in 1992 and addressed simply "*Señores* D.E.A."

"[B]efore sunrise, one of the planes that transports cocaine crashed when it couldn't reach the runway on the Rancho Maya," reads the document which the peasants either signed or inked with their thumbprints. The document names the military commissioners along with seven local officers, including four local army colonels whom the farmers said supervised them.

One of the civilian military commissioners the peasants named was *Rancho Maya* owner Byron Berganza. More than a decade later, in 2004, DEA special agents finally arrested Berganza, along with another Guatemalan civilian, on federal "narcotics importation conspiracy" charges in New York City. Last year, the DEA in Mexico City also helped arrest another Guatemalan, Otto Herrera, who ran a vast trucking fleet from the Zacapa area. Then–Attorney General John Ashcroft described Herrera as one of "the most significant international drug traffickers and money launderers in the world."

Yet, not long after his arrest, Herrera somehow managed to escape from jail in Mexico City. Not one of the Guatemalan military officers the farmers mentioned in their 1992 petition has ever been charged. As the DEA's Senior Special Agent Glaspy explained, "There is a difference between receiving information and being able to prosecute somebody."

U.S. Action

In 2002, then-Chairman Ballenger forced the Bush administration to take limited action to penalize top Guatemalan military officials thought to be involved in drug trafficking. "The visa of former Guatemalan intelligence chief Francisco Ortega Menaldo was revoked," confirmed State Department spokesman Richard A. Boucher in March 2002, "under a section of the Immigration and Nationality Act related to narco-trafficking, and that's about as far as I can go into the details of the decision."

By then, Ret. Gen. Ortega Menaldo had already denied the U.S. drug charges, while reminding reporters in Guatemala City that he had previously collaborated with both the CIA and the DEA dating back to the 1980s. Indeed, a White House

Intelligence Oversight Board has already confirmed that both the CIA and the DEA maintained at least a liaison relationship with Guatemalan military intelligence in the late 1980s and early 1990s when it was run by Col. Ortega Menaldo.

The CIA, through spokesman Mark Mansfield, declined all comment for this article.

Eight months after revoking Ortega Menaldo's visa, the Bush administration again cited suspected drug trafficking to revoke the U.S. entry visa of another Guatemalan intelligence chief, Ret. Gen. Callejas y Callejas. But after the news broke in the Guatemalan press, this *cofradía* officer never responded publicly, as Ortega Menaldo did, to the U.S. drug allegation.

No Civilian Oversight

Rather than confront the impunity that allows Guatemalan military officers to traffic drugs, many of the country's elected officials seem to be going in the opposite direction. Not long after the Bush administration named the two retired cofradía intelligence chiefs as suspected drug traffickers, members of the Guatemalan Republican Front, or FRG party, which was founded by another retired army general, introduced legislation in the Guatemalan Congress that would remove civilian oversight over the military in criminal justice matters.

Throughout the Cold War period, Guatemala's civil justice system seldom had the opportunity to try officers for any crime. Instead officials submitted themselves to military tribunals. In the 1990s, civilian courts began for the first time tentatively to exert their authority to process military officers for crimes like drug trafficking. But the proposed legislation stipulates that any officer, whether active duty or retired, may only be tried in a military tribunal, no matter what the alleged crime. A court martial is normally reserved for crimes allegedly committed by military personnel in the course of their service. If this law is passed, however, it would ensure that

Guatemalan officers accused of any crime, from murder to drug trafficking, could once again only be tried by their military peers.

"This would be a new mechanism of impunity," noted José Zeitune of the Geneva-based International Commission of Jurists and author of a 2005 report on the Guatemalan judiciary.

A Family Affair

As Chairman, Ballenger accused the FRG party, which enjoys a plurality in the Guatemalan Congress, of drug corruption. The FRG was founded by Ret. Gen. Efrain Ríos Montt. A controversial figure, he launched a coup d'etat in 1982 to become president of Guatemala just as the intelligence officers of *la cofradía* were rising.

The new vice-chairman of the Western Hemisphere subcommittee is Jerry Weller III, a Republican from Illinois. He recently married Zury Ríos Sosa, who is Ret. Gen. Montt's daughter. Unlike other members of the Subcommittee, Weller, through his spokesman, Telly Lovelace, declined all comment for this article.

Congressman Weller's father-in-law groomed Guatemala's last president, an FRG member named Alfonso Portillo, who fled the country in 2004 to escape his own arrest for alleged money laundering, according to a State Department report. During President Portillo's tenure, one of his closest companions inside the National Palace was the *cofradía* co-founder Ortega Menaldo, according to Guatemalan press accounts.

A U.N. Investigation?

Today the shadowy structures of Guatemala's intelligence commands are so embedded with organized crime that the Bush administration, for one, is already calling in the United Nations. Putting aside its usual criticisms of the international body, the administration supports a proposal to form a U.N.-led task force explicitly called the "Commission for the Investigation of Illegal Armed Groups and Clandestine Security Apparatus" in Guatemala. So far the only nation to yield its sovereignty to allow the United Nations a similar role is Lebanon, where U.N. investigators are digging into the murder of a former prime minister.

The proposed U.N. plan for Guatemala also enjoys the support of its new president, Oscar Berger, a wealthy landowner and lawyer who is well respected by the U.S. administration. But the proposed U.N. Commission is encountering resistance from FRG politicians like Weller's wife, Ríos Sosa, who is also an FRG congresswoman.

Continued Inaction

So what are U.S. officials and Guatemalan authorities doing to stop the military officers involved in drug trafficking?

"In terms of public corruption against both the army and others, [Guatemalan authorities] have a number of investigations underway, right now," then–Assistant Secretary Robert B. Charles said earlier this year at a State Department press conference. But, in keeping with past practices, not one of these suspected officers has been charged in either Guatemala or the United States.

More troubling still is a recent case involving those Mexican soldiers-turned-hitmen, the Zetas. This past October 22 [2005], seven members of the Zetas were arrested in a Guatemalan border town with weapons and cocaine. The Associated Press reported that, according to Guatemalan authorities, the Zetas came to avenge one of their members who had been killed in Guatemala. Despite the evidence against the men, a little more than a week after their arrests, Guatemalan authorities inexplicably set them free.

The War on Drugs Hurts Poor Colombian Farmers

Garry Leech

Garry Leech is the editor of Colombia Journal *and the author of the book* Killing Peace: Colombia's Conflict and the Failure of U.S. Intervention.

Cecilia walked around her small wooden house pointing to the banana trees and yucca plants that were killed by the aerial fumigation that had occurred eight days earlier. She described how the chemicals blanketed not only the coca crops she and her husband cultivate in order to survive, but also their food crops and two young children. As a result, the family is now struggling to survive in a part of Colombia that has been Cecilia's home for her entire life: the Macarena National Park. Based on the results of the initial fumigations, it appears that Colombian President Alvaro Uribe's decision to begin spraying coca crops in the country's national parks will only intensify the conflict, escalate the humanitarian crisis and increase ecological damage in some of Colombia's most pristine environments.

Macarena National Park

The Macarena National Park is situated east of the Andes Mountains in the department of Meta where the wide-open plains of the north, known as Los Llanos, meet the Amazon Rainforest to the south. The park itself is a spectacular mountainous outcropping covered in lush rainforest and filled with rivers and canyons, much of which is only accessible to the hardiest of travelers. In 1989, the Colombian government finally designated this natural wonder a national park, while

Garry Leech, "Waging War in Colombia's National Parks," *Colombia Journal Online*, September 3, 2006. Reproduced by permission.

UNESCO [United Nations Educational, Scientific and Cultural Organization] declared it a "heritage of humanity" site.

While the interior of the park is mostly uninhabited, several thousand peasants who colonized the region in the 30 years prior to the creation of the park continue to live within its confines—a common practice in Colombia's national parks. The original settlers were peasants fleeing government repression in the 1950s and early 1960s, during the period known as *La Violencia*. The self-defense movements formed by the displaced peasants, in order to protect their lands and families from the Colombian army, eventually became the Revolutionary Armed Forces of Colombia (FARC) in 1966. And now, 40 years later, FARC guerrillas still control the Macarena National Park and its surrounding environs.

The FARC

It is impossible to accurately describe life in the Macarena without discussing the role of the FARC. Not only because the guerrillas profit from the cultivation of coca—a fact repeatedly emphasized by the U.S. and Colombian governments—but also because they are so organically linked to the local peasant population—a fact that the same governments choose to ignore. The conditions that caused peasants to colonize the Colombian Amazon and form the FARC almost a half-century ago still exist in the Macarena today. It is an area that has been grossly neglected by the state in every conceivable manner but one: military repression. The only national government presence in the region has consisted of aerial bombings, short-lived military offensives and now aerial fumigations.

Over the past 50 years, with no support from the national government, the local peasant population has carved a network of primitive dirt roads throughout the rainforest that are only traversable in four-wheel drive vehicles. They have constructed electrical grids powered by gasoline generators for their villages and small towns. And it is the FARC that has become their government, providing such public services as security, social aid and a justice system among other things.

The U.S.-backed Plan Colombia['s] ... targeting of coca crops in southern Colombia has led to a disbursement of coca cultivation throughout the country.

Unlike in some other regions of Colombia where the FARC—and the military and right-wing paramilitaries—impose their rule on local populations, the guerrillas in the Macarena are clearly a government "of the people." Many households in the region have at least one family member in the FARC and the local population interacts with the rebels as naturally and comfortably as rural citizens in the global North do with their local government officials and law enforcement officers. As one peasant explains, "When someone has a problem with another person, perhaps a fight or something, they can take their complaint to the FARC. The FARC then investigates and determines who is at fault and what the sentence will be." He goes on to point out that there are no prisons under the rebels, that the sentences handed down to guilty parties include repairing the roads or working in the fields of communal farms.

Coca Farming

For the most part, peasants have managed to survive in the Macarena region through subsistence farming, including raising cows, pigs and chickens, and growing various food crops such as bananas, yucca, papaya and avocados. It was only 20 years ago that small-scale coca cultivation entered the mix in order to allow peasant families to compensate for the lack of infrastructure, which prevented them from being able to transport their food crops to distant markets. It is only during the past five years, however, that the coca plant has become the most prominent crop in the Macarena region. Farmers grow the coca plants, harvest the leaves and process them into coca paste for sale to drug traffickers, who then process the paste into cocaine. The FARC profits from coca cultivation in the Macarena by taking a cut of all drug transactions in the region.

The recent escalation in coca cultivation in the Macarena has coincided with the implementation of the U.S.-backed Plan Colombia, whose targeting of coca crops in southern Colombia has led to a disbursement of coca cultivation throughout the country. In order to respond to this shift in cultivation patterns, U.S counternarcotics officials began urging President Uribe to approve aerial fumigations of Colombia's national parks, which had remained exempt from spraying operations.

Nearly all of the coca . . . is cultivated by local peasants on small farms of 12 acres or less.

Instead of authorizing aerial fumigations, Uribe announced an alternative plan in December 2005 to send 1,000 manual eradicators under the protection of 3,500 troops to the Macarena National Park. In the ensuing months, more than a dozen military personnel were killed in rebel attacks. In response, the military launched aerial bombardments against FARC positions in the park. The hardship of life in the remotely located park and repeated FARC attacks against the eradication operation eventually caused many of the eradicators to quit and return to their homes outside the region. Finally, after the deaths of six eradicators on August 2 [2006], Uribe gave the order to begin aerial fumigations of coca crops in Macarena National Park.

Aerial Fumigation

Within days, U.S.-supplied spray planes and helicopter gunships began fumigation operations in the coca growing areas of the park, spraying a chemical concoction that has never been approved for use in the United States: the herbicide glyphosate mixed with the surfactant Cosmo Flux 411-F and other additives. After a week of spraying, Colombia's antinarcotics police claimed to have destroyed all 11,370 acres of coca in the park.

It soon became apparent that the Colombian government had exaggerated the success of the aerial fumigation operation; at least in the section of the park visited by this writer eight days after the spraying had ended. While most of the coca had been sprayed, approximately 20 percent remained untouched. Additionally, peasants had saved some of the fumigated coca crops by cutting the tops off the plants before the chemicals could destroy the roots. As a result, these plants will continue to produce five harvests of coca leaves annually. Meanwhile, the spraying also killed many small trees and bushes in the rainforest perimeter around the coca fields.

While fast-acting peasants can save their coca crops by cutting them at the stem, the same process is ineffective on less-hardy food crops such as banana, papaya and avocado trees, and smaller plants including yucca. Nearly all of the coca in the Macarena region is cultivated by local peasants on small farms of 12 acres or less. The money these farmers earn from their coca crops allows them to supplement the food that they grow with other necessities. Consequently, because the cultivation of coca does not provide them with much disposable income, the destruction of food crops has caused a major food crisis for many households.

Additionally, many family members and hired coca pickers were present on the farms when the spraying indiscriminately targeted homes situated in the midst of food and coca crops. As a result, many children and coca pickers, who earn approximately $10 a day harvesting coca, were sprayed with chemicals that caused them to suffer from various gastrointestinal problems. Cecilia described how her two children both began vomiting shortly after the spraying and then suffered from diarrhea for several days.

'The fumigations hurt the peasants more than the guerrillas. They are the ones who are most dependent on coca for their survival'.

Children also suffered psychological trauma from the militaristic nature of the fumigation operation. Helicopter gunships swooped down low over farms only minutes ahead of the spray planes to unleash barrages of machine gun fire around the perimeter of coca fields. The earth is pockmarked with holes created by bullets from the machine guns while hundreds of shell casings litter the ground, often dangerously close to homes.

Fighting the FARC

The U.S. and Colombian governments claim that destroying coca crops in the FARC-controlled Macarena will diminish the funding that the rebel group receives from the illegal drug trade, thereby weakening it militarily. Colombia's Defense Minister Camilo Ospina explained the military objective of the coca eradication campaign, "We cannot pretend that eliminating the checkbook of the guerrillas will be an easy process. The process in La Macarena consists of the eradication of coca in one of the zones of the world with the greatest levels of cultivation, which represents the most important source of financing for subversive groups, specifically the FARC."

For its part, the Bush administration expressed its satisfaction with President Uribe's response to its repeated requests that spray planes be deployed to Colombia's national parks. James O'Gara of the White House's Office of National Drug Control Policy declared, "If the FARC thought the government would allow coca to grow untrammeled in its national parks, they've obviously miscalculated." But according to a local FARC commander, "The fumigations hurt the peasants more than the guerrillas. They are the ones who are most dependent on coca for their survival." While the fumigations are probably affecting the FARC's finances to some degree, more than six years of Plan Colombia has provided little evidence that this strategy is noticeably weakening the rebel group's military capacity. If anything, such tactics are only further entrenching popular support for the guerrillas in remote regions of the country such as the Macarena.

It is unlikely that [aerial] fumigations will eliminate coca cultivation.

In addition to Plan Colombia's counternarcotics operations, the Colombian military has also been implementing the U.S.-backed Plan Patriota, a large-scale counterinsurgency operation intended to seize control of FARC-controlled areas in southern and eastern Colombia, including the Macarena region. But Plan Patriota has proved ineffective, often only consisting of sporadic ground offensives into FARC-controlled areas. According to peasants in the Macarena region, the army often kills civilians during these incursions and then publicly blames the FARC—accusations that are then dutifully reported by the national and international media without any investigation into the crimes.

There have also been several incidents under Plan Patriota of peasants in the Macarena region being arbitrarily arrested by Colombian troops and taken to the army base in Vista Hermosa, located on the side of the Guapaya River controlled by the state. In one incident that occurred in January 2006, the army rounded up eight peasants and took them to the military base. Officials claim that all of those detained were later released although only one of them has since been seen. The other seven were likely "disappeared" by right-wing paramilitaries who, according to several residents in Vista Hermosa, are still active in the area despite their supposed demobilization.

The situation for the peasants living in the Macarena has changed little since they settled the region some 50 years ago. To this day, the policies of the national government in Bogotá have only consisted of military operations that have often resulted in gross violations of human rights. Under Uribe's Plan Patriota, there has been no attempt to provide peasants who have traditionally lived in rebel-controlled regions with any social or economic programs in order to win the battle for the "hearts and minds" of the local population. . . .

With the complete failure of the government to even attempt to provide any basic services to the local population, it is the FARC that has filled the void by helping to build roads and provide electricity, law enforcement, judges and other public services traditionally supplied by the state. As one local peasant notes, "When farmers or their families get sick and can't afford medicine, it is the FARC that gives them money to purchase what they need."

The peasant population of the Macarena region sees no reason to trust a government that has offered them nothing but repression, or at best, total neglect. In August [2006], the government ensured that this distrust would become further entrenched by launching a militarized fumigation campaign that made children sick while destroying essential food crops. Once again, it is the civilian population that has been victimized by the government's counterinsurgency strategy. For the local peasant population, the only ones they can turn to for help are the guerrillas, which undermines the very counterinsurgency objectives that the government should be trying to achieve: winning the hearts and minds of the people.

Fumigation Will Fail

Ultimately, it is unlikely that the fumigations will eliminate coca cultivation in the Macarena region. A significant percentage of the crops survived the spraying and many of those that were destroyed will simply be replaced with new ones. Sometimes this replanting will take place on the same plots of land, other times peasants will cut down more rainforest in order to replant. But as one farmer points out, "If you simply start cutting down trees to plant more crops, the FARC will fine you. We must obtain permission from the guerrillas before we can cut down the rainforest." It is not always easy to obtain that permission because the FARC is attempting to carry out a balancing act between funding its insurgency from coca cultivation, allowing peasants to earn a living, and limiting the destruction of one of the country's most exquisite ecological treasures.

There is no evidence that the Colombian government is willing to attempt a balancing act of its own in order to implement a more comprehensive counterinsurgency strategy. Until the government offers peasants like Cecilia something more than military repression, the local populations in areas such as the Macarena will continue to see their welfare and survival as inextricably intertwined with that of the FARC. Consequently, violence will continue to wreak havoc on another of the country's national treasures: its people.

Legalizing Drugs Would Improve the Situation in Colombia

Toby Muse

Toby Muse is a freelance journalist based in Bogota, Colombia.

Everyone remember the small plane that buzzed around the clear sky over this beautiful section of western Colombia toward the end of 2003, tossing out hundreds of pamphlets. Promising a "black Christmas," the pamphlets said "the good children will go to bed early. The bad children we'll put to bed ourselves." Colombia's worst drug war in more than a decade was about to get worse.

Set amid rich farmland in the shadows of mountains, the towns of El Dovio, Zarzal, and Roldanillo are snapshots of rustic Colombia's beauty. Middle-aged women, overweight in that way peculiar to a rich rural diet, can be seen driving the latest SUVs. Behind this rural gentility, these towns have long served as the headquarters of Colombia's largest remaining cocaine trafficking organization, the Northern Valley cartel. The cartel is at war with itself, a firestorm of violence targeting anyone linked to the organization in the past or present, no matter how tenuously.

Brutal Violence

In this tiny corner of Columbia, with a population of 260,000, more than 1,000 people have been murdered during the last 20 months [from 2005 to 2007]. The war is between former partners within the cartel, one of whom, Diego Montoya, sits alongside Osama bin Laden on the FBI's [Federal Bureau of

Toby Muse, "Legalization Now!: War-Weary Colombia—and Its Conservative Party—Consider Ending the Drug War," *Reason*, vol. 37, June 2005 p. 32–38. Copyright 2005 by Reason Foundation, 3415 S. Sepulveda Blvd., Suite 400, Los Angeles, CA 90034, www.reason.com. Reproduced by permission.

Investigation] top-10 wanted list. According to police, the war began when each capo [head of a branch of a crime syndicate] began worrying that the others might be planning to negotiate with the Colombian and U.S. authorities at the expense of their associates.

The war has followed the cartel's trail across Colombia, with a series of grisly killings in the country's principal cities: Bogota, Cali, and Medellin. The war's cruelty has shocked a country that thought it was desensitized to violence. Victims have been asphyxiated with plastic bags, killed by nails hammered into their heads, and in some cases dismembered while still alive.

The authorities are struggling to cope with the underage assassins carrying out many of these killings. Since the most popular form of assassination involves a shooter sitting on the back of a high-powered motorbike, some Colombian cities made it illegal for two men to travel on the same motorbike. The assassins responded by putting wigs on the shooters to make them look like women.

"This drug war has moved beyond a question of crime," says Apolinar Salcedo, the mayor of Cali, Colombia's second largest city and the scene of much of the killing. "This is now a question of national security."

Cocaine violence, combined with endemic poverty, has given Colombia one of the world's highest murder rates.

Legalization Now

This hurricane of violence has led a growing number of Colombians, including leading members of the venerable Conservative Party, to question the drug policies that have helped make their country one of the world's most dangerous. "We Colombians have had enough," says Ferney Lozano, director of the Legalization Now movement, which was founded in 1999 and claims more than 100 elected officials across the country as members. "We're sick of paying the consequences of this war against drugs with thousands killed each year. People are seeing that if anything things are getting worse, with more people becoming addicts, and they are now questioning whether the costs of this drug war are worth it."

Legalization Now says the money spent waging the War on Drugs should instead be spent on rehabilitation for drug addicts and aid to coca farmers to help them switch crops. The changes advocated by Colombia's reformers range from decriminalization, which would lift all penalties on drug possession, to the worldwide repeal of prohibition, which would eliminate the drug trade's artificially inflated profits and put the traffickers out of business. By itself Colombia can do only so much, since both demand for cocaine and the demand to eliminate its production come from abroad. But criticism of the War on Drugs from members of the country's political establishment shows that President Alvaro Uribe's gungho support for U.S. anti-drug efforts is not the only respectable position. "To be honest," says Lozano, "I think before 10 years it's highly unlikely that we'll see a change in the drugs policy, but we've made huge advances in the five years we've been working."

Drug Warriors

Cocaine violence, combined with endemic poverty, has given Colombia one of the world's highest murder rates. The violence does not stop with the cartels: The illicit drug trade is the main source of funding for the country's four-decade civil war, which pits Marxist guerrillas against extreme right-wing paramilitaries and the state.

The right-wing United Self-Defense Forces of Colombia, known by their Spanish acronym AUC, have grown to become the most important illegal armed group in the country, eclipsing even the guerrillas as they've consolidated power in different regions, taking over local governments and reaching as high as the Colombian Congress. The rapid growth was funded both by contributions from legal businesses and by drug profits; according to a former head of the AUC, 70 percent of the group's income comes from drugs.

Colombia's economy has suffered as a result of the drug trade.

In 2003 a rogue AUC commander known as Double Zero attempted to lead a rebellion within the paramilitaries against the drug traffickers. "The paramilitaries lost their way," he told me in early 2004, "Instead of concentrating on defeating the guerrillas, they've become dedicated to nothing more than drug trafficking." In a match between ideals and drug money, ideals were crushed. Double Zero's bloc was annihilated and he himself assassinated. The drug trafficking wing of the paramilitaries was supreme. In a reflection of how high the traffickers reach in the movement, six of the 14 commanders in peace talks with the government have extradition warrants out for them, including the current leader, Salvatore Mancuso. They all deny dealing drugs.

Cocaine also funds their enemies, the Marxist guerrillas. The U.S. and Colombian governments claim the 20,000-strong Revolutionary Armed Forces of Colombia (known by its Spanish acronym, FARC) earns hundreds of millions of dollars a year from the drug trade. A number of FARC guerrillas face extradition warrants, and the highest-ranking leader ever captured was sent to the U.S. over Christmas to stand trial on drug trafficking charges.

FARC denies any participation in the drug trade, insisting it only taxes coca farmers. FARC's other main source of income is kidnapping, helping propel Colombia to the top spot on the world's kidnapping index.

FARC's actions suggest a growing interest in drug trafficking to finance the revolution. FARC has targeted paramilitary coca fields, killing peasants working there. It's no coincidence that the civil war is most heavily contested where coca is grown and along the borders, where control of territory allows the export of drugs and import of arms.

Who Profits?

While bearing the brunt of prohibition-related violence, most Colombians have not benefited much from black market profits. The U.N. [United Nations] estimates that the drug trade may account for as little as 1 percent of the country's GDP [gross domestic product] placing it below oil. The product itself is cheap until it arrives in the U.S.; most of the profits are made outside of Colombia.

Francisco Thoumi, an economics professor at Bogota's Rosario University who has published a number of books on the cocaine industry, says Colombia's economy has suffered as a result of the drug trade. "In the 1980s," he says, "the rate of homicides skyrocketed, and that made investments too risky for many companies." The attitudes encouraged by the drug trade also have hurt the economy. "It becomes impossible to do business because everyone distrusts everyone else," says Thoumi, "so everyone is playing defensive and not willing to take any sort of risk."

Colombians have an ambivalent attitude toward the drug industry. In the old cocaine centers of Cali and Medellin, billions of inflowing dollars funded a boom that lined everyone's pockets during the 1980s and '90s. Tellingly, when the Cali drug lords were arrested the city's construction industry virtually ground to a halt. In Medellin during the '80s, a popular way for otherwise law-abiding people to make almost guaranteed profits was to buy a stake in a shipment of cocaine from drug lords seeking to spread the risk of seizure.

Even today, drug money and drug traffickers hang at the edges of legitimate society. Although members of the upper classes are not above profiting from the cocaine trade, they look down on the narcos in the same way that wealthy people the world over disdain the nouveau riche [newly rich]. The narcos' propensity for gold-plated toilets, bejeweled prostitutes, and loud parties has not endeared them to their neighbors in the fashionable districts.

Among many of Colombia's poor, by contrast, drugs are seen as a way to earn money in an economy where more than 60 percent of the population lives on or below the poverty line. The Medellin carters Pablo Escobar, after all, started out stealing gravestones before entering the cocaine trade and becoming one of the world's richest men. Admiration for the industry is reflected in a genre of music popular in Colombia's poorer neighborhoods that features songs with titles like "I Prefer a Tomb in Colombia (to a Jail in the U.S.)" and "The Cartels Are Still Alive."

Support for Legalization

Surveys indicate that public support for legalization has grown since Legalization Now was founded five years ago, when it hovered around 7 percent. A poll taken in July 2003 by Invamer-Gallup showed 22 percent national support for "the legalization of production and consumption of drugs." What was more interesting was how the figures broke down. In the capital, 27 percent of people were in favor, while in the historic centers of the cocaine cartels, Medellin and Cali, the numbers were 16 percent and 13 percent, respectively. Responses also varied by class, with nearly 40 percent of Colombia's upper classes supporting legalization, compared to 16 percent of Colombia's lowest social strata.

"We have found that it's an educational difference," says Legalization Now's Lozano. "Poorer neighborhoods often are more against this because they believe that as soon as we legalize everyone will immediately become addicts. We've got to educate these people that the current approach is not working and if you really want to protect your children, you must help legalize drugs."

Colombia has changed from a producing country where drug use was frowned upon and drugs were a gringo problem, to a producing and consuming country. Authorities say that in recent years the cartels noticed the virgin market at home and started a drive for greater sales in Colombia. Studies show that Colombian children are starting drugs younger, and a trip to any of the country's city centers finds homeless children passed out midday with a bag of bazuco, a cheap drug made from the remnants of cocaine production. Legalization Now estimates that of Colombia's 45 million inhabitants, some 5 million are regular drug users.

Unexpected Reformers

Proponents of drug legalization are often accused of being in the pay of the drug lords, a testament to the power the narcos wielded in the past, especially in Colombia's Congress. (One former president became synonymous with corruption after it was found that the Call cartel helped bankroll his campaign.) President Uribe recently ripped open the debate again, accusing M-19, a now defunct guerrilla group, of working with the drug traffickers. In the scandal that erupted, prominent congressmen who had belonged to M-19 and had in the past spoken favorably of legalization said they would no longer talk about the issue for fear of further being associated with the drug traffickers.

"I've been calling for legalization for 20 years, and I can't remember the [number] of times I've been called in the pockets of the drug lords," says Antonio Caballero, one of Colombia's most famous columnists, who writes for the country's largest news magazine, *Semana*. "Of course, it doesn't make any sense, because it's the drug lords who will be out of business if there is legalization, but it does help shut down the discussion."

When Gustavo de Grieff, then Colombia's prosecutor general, started criticizing the War on Drugs in the 1990s, he likewise was tarred as a tool of the traffickers, even though he had led the successful effort to shut down Escobar's murderous Medellin cartel. In 1994 Sen. John Kerry (D-Mass.) wrote a *Washington Post* op-ed piece in which he said De Grieff's "positions are nearly identical with those of the (Cali) cartel itself. As such, they demonstrate the degree to which the Cali cartel has already gained influence in the very offices of Colombian law enforcement that are supposed to protect society against the cartel."

'To produce a gram of salt or sugar is more expensive than [producing] a gram of cocaine.'

But as the suffering of Colombia continues in this brutal War on Drugs, an irreproachable group is stepping forward to call for a review of the country's drug policies. Colombia's Conservative Party is very conservative indeed. Founded in 1849, it earned a reputation for ferocious religious violence during Colombia's various civil wars between the conservatives and liberals. A poster in party headquarters listing its goals and policies ends with the highlighted words "a party that believes in God and seeks to insert him into life." More than half of Colombia's presidents have come from the Conservative Party, which in many eyes is associated with landowners, the church, and the oligarchy. Yet this bastion of conservatism is now mulling the decriminalization of drugs.

Decriminalizing Drugs

Enrique Gomez Hurtado comes from an illustrious political dynasty. His brother was assassinated while running for president on a right-wing ticket. In his congressional office sits a bust of his father, a president in the middle of the last century. Gomez Hurtado belongs to a class of Colombians who resemble English gentlemen of the Victorian era. On the wall of his office hangs a copy of the Ten Commandments. He is proposing the decriminalization of drugs as a way of dealing with Colombia's problems as both a drug-producing and a drug-consuming nation.

"We know that the industry is profitable only because it is illegal, and the day that tobacco becomes outlawed, that will take cocaine's place as the largest mafia business," Gomez Hurtado says, sitting at a desk on which a stack of pamphlets outlining his case for decriminalization is neatly piled. "To produce a gram of salt or sugar is more expensive than (producing) a gram of cocaine. The difference in final price only comes because cocaine is illegal."

Gomez Hurtado is asking his party to agree on a platform that includes decriminalization of drugs in Colombia, rather than outright legalization, and a shift of government resources from aggressive anti-drug policies to rehabilitation, "Legalization would show indifference in front of this illness of drug addiction," he says. "It would be like legalizing tuberculosis or AIDS. You can't legalize a disease." He recognizes that Colombia alone cannot eliminate the black market in cocaine. "We need greater help in reviewing international policies towards drugs," he says, "because this is economics; the supply comes from the demand."

Legalizing Alone?

Conservative support for the decriminalization or legalization of drugs is based largely on the belief that Colombia fights alone on the front line of the War on Drugs and that as a result the entire country has become a battlefield. All this for a war demanded by other countries, most conspicuously the United States. Drugs are so profitable because they are illegal and in great demand among those who can afford them. Nearly 75 percent of the world's cocaine is consumed in North America and Western Europe.

"I share Colombians' frustration," says Sandro Calvani, director of the United Nations International Drug Control Program in Bogota. "They pay with all the violence of the war, yet the consuming countries don't share the burden. Some European countries don't even help Colombia with one peso."

But Calvani is hesitant about extrapolating from the experience of other countries that have experimented with more tolerant drug policies. "Where they've done this, such as Holland and Switzerland, there has been a history of liberal thinking and high levels of education among the population," he says. About one in 10 Colombians is illiterate, and that rate rises sharply in the countryside, where children are often taken out of school to work.

Colombian supporters of drug policy reform are concerned about the international reaction to their proposals. "We cannot become a pariah state, and that is what would happen if we legalized alone," says Sen. Carlos Holguin, leader of the Conservative Party, who is spoken of as a possible presidential candidate. "It would make no sense, because it's not so much the problem here, but the problem is that they're illegal outside. It should be a policy of the Colombian government to pressure the international community to force them to review their drug policies. We must look at this as a health issue."

Coca farmers . . . have a monthly profit of 400,000 pesos, just over $150.

Fumigation

Many opponents of the drug war think its environmental cost is reason enough to abandon it. The cornerstone of Colombia's U.S.-funded anti-drug effort is aerial fumigation. The U.S. and

Colombian governments have been celebrating the success of the fumigation program. The U.N. reported that in 2003 the number of hectares devoted to coca cultivation fell 16 percent, to 86,000, the lowest level since 1997. President Uribe recently estimated that the country would have less than 65,000 hectares of coca by the end of this year. "Sixty-five thousand hectares is immense, and the political aim has to be zero land devoted to drug crops in Colombia," he said.

Fumigation missions will cost some $100 million this year. As coca production has spread to encompass much of Colombian territory—satellites even pick up images of coca fields near the capital—so have fumigations. Residents and environmentalists protested the fumigation of Colombia's national parks, including the Sierra Nevada, the world's highest coastal range. Indigenous tribes who live there complain that the fumigations are polluting the rivers and killing legal crops. The U.S. and Colombian governments insist the fumigations, which use the herbicide glyphosate, are safe. Farmers living in fumigated areas complain of myriad sicknesses, including skin problems and birth defects.

Pedro Arenas is head of the leftist Communal and Communitarian Movement and congressman for the Department of Guaviare, one of the biggest coca-producing regions. Not coincidentally, it is also the site of the government's largest-ever offensive against the FARC rebels. "We're seeing in this drug war the militarization of our communities, and peasants becoming enemies of the state," Arenas says. Although the official numbers show a decline in coca production, he says, the coca farmers in his department have told him they think it is rising. Farmers are shielding coca from satellites by planting more trees. Any potential decline in land given over to coca production is offset by the increasing use of a coca strain that can be harvested more often and produces more cocaine per plant. Critics of the eradication program also point to a "balloon effect": As production is pushed down in one area, it pops up elsewhere. Peru's anti-drug agency estimated that the country produced 160 tons of cocaine in 2004, one-fifth more than in 2003, and another increase is expected this year [2005].

Drug traffickers normally outsource the production of coca to the farmers, who grow the coca and take the initial steps in processing it into blocks of coca paste, which are then purchased by the traffickers and turned into cocaine. "These fumigations are going after the lowest people on the chain," says Arenas. "These farmers need to live, and they see no alternative but coca." He estimates the coca farmers, known as *cocaleros*, have a monthly profit of 400,000 pesos, just over $150. "These fumigations are destroying our environment," he says, "because every time they fumigate fields, the peasants plant again on new land, and they're moving deeper into the jungles."

Many Colombians and foreign observers feel fumigations treat the symptom rather than the underlying illness. While the poverty that propels farmers to plant coca remains, any attempt to stop them from doing so will in all likelihood be futile. "At the moment, we're spending around $5,000 per hectare fumigated," says the U.N.'s Sergio Calvani. "If that money could be distributed among the peasants, then Colombia would be like Switzerland."

An Uphill Battle

The government of Alvaro Uribe, a member of the Liberal Party and Washington's closest ally in South America, has avoided any discussion of decriminalizing drugs. In fact, the president backed an unsuccessful referendum that would have overturned the current laws that allow possession of drugs for personal use. His supporters in Washington say Uribe is the president Colombia has long needed, praising his offensive against the Marxist rebels and the drug industry. Uribe has boosted the army and the police and struck at the FARC's traditional stronghold in the south.

The relationship between Uribe and President [George W.] Bush "could not be closer," says Kimberly Stanton, deputy director of the Washington Office on Latin America, an organization that opposes fumigation and argues that the war on drugs is counterproductive. Bush paid Uribe a compliment by visiting Colombia on his first trip abroad following his re-election.

In any case, says Stanton, "There is no way the U.S. will allow the Colombian Congress to adopt legalization. It will do everything in its power to stop this, I assure you." The U.S. is the largest donor of aid to Colombia, takes about half of Colombia's exports, and has tremendous influence on multilateral institutions that lend vital money to the cash-strapped central government. Colombia has become increasingly dependent on U.S. aid for its war against the Marxist guerrillas, the right-wing paramilitaries, and of course the drug industry. The country has received nearly $4 billion from the U.S. since the launch of the huge anti-drug initiative Plan Colombia in 2000.

"Way too many Colombian leaders think that unless they do everything the U.S. wants they'll lose everything," says Stanton, adding that Colombia should propose a review of global anti-drug policies. As the drug violence continues and the deaths mount, Colombia's population may just force their leaders to stand up and demand from the world a change in global drug policies.

CHAPTER 4

Are Efforts to Stop Drug Trafficking Helping the War on Terror?

Chapter Preface

Afghanistan has one of the worst opium problems in the world. One million Afghans—one in every thirty-two citizens of the country—is thought to be addicted to the drug. According to an estimate prepared by the United Nations, more than half of these addicts are children under age fifteen. A number of those addicts are infants: In some parts of Afghanistan, it has become a common practice to give babies opium to stop them from crying and to encourage them to sleep.

This is not the "opium problem" that normally comes to mind when foreigners think about Afghanistan. To the rest of the world, talk about drugs and Afghanistan usually centers on the heroin trade, in which Afghanistan has become a major player in the past few decades. (Opium and heroin are both made from the sap of the same opium poppies; heroin is simply a more refined form of the drug.) By some estimates, today as much as 90 percent of the world's heroin supply is made from opium poppies grown in Afghanistan.

This was not always the case. Historically the major center of opium production in Asia was the so-called Golden Triangle, the area where Myanmar, Laos, and Thailand come together. This area was known for wars and political instability, which made it difficult for governments in the area to crack down on drug trafficking. In recent decades, this region and Afghanistan have switched: The countries of the Golden Triangle have become more stable and have been able to stop most heroin production in that area, while Afghanistan has become less politically stable and has seen its opium production explode.

Afghanistan's political problems began in 1978, when a Communist coup overthrew the royal family that had ruled Afghanistan for hundreds of years. The new Communist government was unpopular, and the situation in Afghanistan soon deteriorated. Late in 1979 the Soviet Union, which bordered Afghanistan to the north, took advantage of the instability to invade the country. The Soviet Union fought against the Afghan rebels known as "mujahedeen" for the next ten years, destroying Afghanistan in the process. Over a million Afghans were killed during the war, and millions more became refugees.

The Soviet Union withdrew from Afghanistan in 1989, but the war continued. Finally, in 1996, one faction managed to take control of most of Afghanistan. This faction, called the Taliban, consisted of fervent Muslims who forced their interpretation of Islam on the rest of the country. They banned entertainment such as films and music, forbade girls from attending school and women from having jobs, and reintroduced the traditional Islamic punishments of amputations and public executions for criminals. The Taliban also provided a safe haven for foreign Islamic militant groups, most notably al Qaeda, which grew out of the groups of foreign Muslims who came to Afghanistan to help fight against the Soviets in the 1980s. The Taliban finally brought a measure of peace to Afghanistan, but they failed to bring prosperity. The Afghan people, most of whom were still mired in poverty, increasingly began growing opium in order to feed their families.

The Taliban was overthrown by the United States in 2001 as part of a U.S. effort to destroy the al Qaeda network in that country, but the political situation in Afghanistan remains precarious and the people remain poor. The American, British, Canadian, and other international forces that continue to occupy the country face the difficult task of defeating the surviving members of the Taliban and the other insurgents who want to overthrow Afghanistan's newly created democratic government. Should those soldiers be ordered to fight against Afghan poppy growers as well or would taking on Afghanistan's drug problem hinder efforts to wipe out the last of the terrorists in Afghanistan? This is one of the questions debated by the authors in this chapter.

Terrorism Around the World Is Funded by Drug Trafficking

Asa Hutchinson

Asa Hutchinson is the former administrator of the U.S. Drug Enforcement Administration.

Let's briefly look at the facts of the connection between drugs and terrorism, starting with Afghanistan. Afghanistan, as you know, is a major source of heroin in the world, producing in the year 2000 some 70 percent of the world's supply of opium, which is converted to heroin.

Afghanistan

The Taliban, the ruling authority at the time, benefited from that drug trade by taxing and, in some instances, being involved in the drug trafficking. Taxation was institutionalized to the extent that they actually issued tax receipts when they collected the revenue from the heroin traffickers.

I read from one receipt that was obtained during one of the operations there: "To the honorable road tax collectors: Gentlemen, the bearer of this letter who possesses four kilograms of white good has paid the custom duty at the Shinwa custom. It is hoped that the bearer will not be bothered further."

So it's clear that the Taliban benefited from the institutionalized taxation of heroin trafficking. Clearly, at the same time, the al-Qaeda network flourished from the safe haven provided by the Taliban.

Taken a step further, the DEA [Drug Enforcement Administration], has also received multi-source information that Osama bin Laden himself has been involved in the financing

Asa Hutchinson, "Narco-Terror: The International Connection Between Drugs and Terror," Heritage Foundation, June 20, 2002. Copyright © 2002 The Heritage Foundation. Reproduced by permission.

and facilitation of hereoin-trafficking activities. That is history now with the operation that has been taking place by our military in Afghanistan.

Since 1990, 73 American citizens have been taken hostage in Colombia, more than 50 by narco-terrorists.

Now we can look to the future in Afghanistan. We're pleased that the interim president, Chairman [Hamid] Karzai, has banned poppy cultivation and drug production; but the United Nations, despite this ban that is currently in place, estimates that the area that is currently under cultivation could potentially produce up to 2,700 metric tons of opium in Afghanistan this coming year. This is an extraordinary concern to the DEA and the international community.

To put this in perspective, when you look at one area of the world producing 2,700 metric tons of opium, that contrasts to less than 100 metric tons of heroin being consumed in the United States. It's an overproduction in supply. It is a huge challenge that we face in Afghanistan, but it is also a tremendous opportunity for the international community to be energized, to be cooperative in their efforts to engage in that arena to impact the huge supply that comes out of Afghanistan.

Colombia

In Colombia, we deal with three groups designated as terrorist organizations by the State Department: the revolutionary group called the FARC (Revolutionary Armed Forces of Colombia); the ELN (National Liberation Army); and a paramilitary group, the AUC (United Self-Defenses of Colombia). At least two of those, without any doubt, are heavily engaged in drug trafficking, receiving enormous funds from drug trafficking: the AUC and the FARC.

In the case of the FARC, the State Department has called them the mast dangerous international terrorist group based in the Western Hemisphere. Two weeks ago, the Department of Justice indicted three members of the 16th Front of the FARC, including their commander, Tomas Molina, on charges of conspiracy to transport cocaine and distribute it in the United States. It was the first time that members of a known terrorist organization have been indicted on drug trafficking charges.

The 16th Front operates out of a remote village in Eastern Colombia where they operate an air strip, where they engage in their trafficking activities, where they control all the operations in that particular arena. The cocaine that is transported by the 16th Front out of that area is paid for with currency, with weapons, and with equipment; and, of course, you know the activities that that terrorist organization has been engaged in, in which they would use that currency, the weapons, and the equipment.

But the 16th Front is not the only front of the FARC that is engaged in drug trafficking activity. Ninety percent of the cocaine Americans consume comes from Colombia; the FARC controls the primary coca cultivation and processing regions in that country, and they have controlled it for the past two decades.

The State Department estimates that the FARC receives $300 million a year from drug sales to finance its terrorist activities.

In March of this year [2002], under the direction of President [Andrés] Pastrana, the Colombian Army and the Colombian National Police reclaimed the demilitarized zone from the FARC, based upon intelligence the DEA was able to provide. The police went in, and in the demilitarized zone that was supposed to be a peaceful haven, they found two major cocaine laboratories. The police seized five tons of processed cocaine from that particular site, so you can imagine the enormity of this processing site. They destroyed the labs as well as a 200-foot communications tower that the FARC operated to use in their communications efforts.

Drugs are a funding source for terrorism and violence.

Prior to the seizure, we knew the FARC was engaged in trafficking activities, but this is the first time we have had solid evidence that the FARC is involved in the cocaine trade from start to finish, from cultivation to processing and distribution.

We should understand that's it's not just Colombian citizens that are impacted by the terrorist activities. Since 1990, 73 American citizens have been taken hostage in Colombia, more than 50 by narco-terrorists; and since 1995, 12 American citizens have been murdered.

So we see a clear connection by al-Qaeda and the FARC using drug proceeds to finance their terrorist activities. They are not by any means the only two groups.

I mentioned the AUC, the paramilitary group in which Carlos Castagna, the leader of that organization, actually published a book in which he admitted that his paramilitary activities, his terrorist activities, were in fact funded to a large extent by drug trafficking. Let me assure you that he is under investigation.

Peru

In Peru, you have the Shining Path. There's evidence that they were responsible for the car bombing that occurred just two weeks ago [June 2002] that killed nine people prior to President [George W.] Bush's visit to Peru. They have historically also benefited from the taxation of coca cultivation in the region of Peru that they control.

So, yes, the facts demonstrate that drugs are a funding source for terrorism and violence against government. But it's not just the facts that are involved here; it's also the lives that are impacted to such an extraordinary extent.

Mexico

When I went to Mexico City in February [2002], I had a meeting with the Attorney General, Macedo de la Concha, and in that meeting, I shook hands with the prosecutors that were on the back row as I was leaving. One of the prosecutors, Mario Roldan Quirino, was handling a case that we were involved in that was a multi-ton seizure of cocaine off of a fishing vessel. I shook hands with that prosecutor. Within one hour after I left Mexico City, Mario Roldan was shot 28 times outside of Mexico City and assassinated. . . .

In the first few months of 2002, 13 law enforcement officers have been murdered in Mexico. You say, "this may not be terrorism." When you're going after government officials, judicial officials, to impact the stability of a government, in my judgment, it is terrorism.

Last week, I visited the Colombian National Police—not just their police building, but also their hospital. In that hospital, I visited with five officers who were wounded in an attack by the FARC while they were doing coca eradication and providing protection for that operation.

Of those five that were wounded, four of these will return to duty. They are pleased to have that level of commitment. One will not return to duty. He was paralyzed for the rest of his life as the result of a car bomb attack near the United States embassy by a terrorist in Bogota. He was 24 years of age. All I could say to that young man was "Thank you."

America's understanding of the cost could best be demonstrated by "Just Say No to Drugs" in the United States.

America's National Interest

What is the national interest when it happens in faraway countries? It should be elementary: Drug production in Mexico, in

Colombia, in Thailand, and in Afghanistan produces the supply of drugs that devastates our families and our communities.

The same illegal drug production funds that attack civilized society also destabilize democracies across the globe. Illegal drug production undermines America's culture; it funds terror; and it erodes democracy. And they all represent a clear and present danger to our national security.

Drug Trafficking Fuels Organized Crime, Civil Wars, and Terrorism

Antonio Maria Costa

Antonio Maria Costa is the executive director of the United Nations Office on Drugs and Crime.

I want to talk to you today about drugs and organized crime. Let me speak plainly: drug dollars are the cash cow on which Transnational Organized Crime relies. It uses the profits from drug trafficking, estimated at 30 billion per year, to bankroll terrorists, capitalize other illegal enterprises, expand criminal markets, and to subsidize war, violence, anarchy and lawlessness.

There are some people who argue with this view.

They claim the transaction between drug trafficker and drug user is simple and straightforward—that it has no broad effect on society, and no lasting impact on anyone but the drug user himself. Wrong. Very wrong. The fact is that the trafficking and use of illegal drugs continues to have a profound impact on everyone's life.

Drug trafficking, drug use, and the illegal proceeds of drug sales distort the world's economies, destroy the lives of entire generations, and decimate populations via HIV/AIDS.

Global Supply and Demand

Let me tell you where we stand today in regard to global supply and demand. Production is down everywhere in the world—with the exception of Afghanistan. Demand in down in the United States, relatively stable in Europe, and growing, unfortunately, in Russia and China.

Just last week [January 2005], I was in Afghanistan to talk to newly elected officials there about drugs and their impact on the Afghan economy and its new democratic government. Today, Afghanistan supplies roughly 87 percent of the world's heroin to millions of consumers across Europe, Central Asia, Russia and the CIS [Commonwealth of Independent States] countries.

Afghanistan is both the largest cultivator of opium in the world, and the world's largest supplier, a double record. In spite of this distinction, only 3 percent of Afghanistan's growing fields are devoted to the cultivation of poppies, and only 10 percent of the population is involved in the drug industry.

Economic Addiction to Drugs

That may not sound like much—but in Afghanistan, the revenue derived from opium is almost *twice* the amount of money the country has been taking in as international aid. An acre of poppies returns 27 times more than an acre of wheat.

Today, narco-dollars account for half of Afghanistan's Gross National Product. That means that opium and heroin are fuelling the Afghan economy—bringing economic development to some of the poorest communities on earth, creating jobs and markets for taxable imports, and restoring hope to people who believe they are lucky to be part of *any* "trickle-down" economy, even one driven by illegal drugs.

Afghanistan is a country where, until recently, most people travelled by donkey, and telephones, electricity, and even indoor plumbing were unknown luxuries. Today those same people are literally trading in their donkeys for shiny new S UV's, loaded with cruise control, AMIFMICD, moon roofs and' satellite navigational systems. The donkey goes into a pen in back of the Land Rover dealership, and a new SUV rolls off the showroom floor. Mountain dwellers who used to signal to one another by hand, or by whistling across great distances, now sport cell phones.

Countries become addicted to drug economies the same way people become addicted to drugs.

In villages and towns, flat-screen televisions, DVD players, boom boxes, motorcycles, Jaguars and Mercedes, are everywhere—symbols of the new, drug-driven prosperity. But here is what is concerns us most—all of these "blessings" flow from a criminal, underground economy in which increasing numbers of Afghan citizens have a real and substantial stake. Intentionally or unintentionally, they have entered into a pact with the devil.

Some people think drug money travels in a straight line—from grower to wholesaler, retailer, consumer, and back again to the farmer in need of seed for a new crop of opium poppies. They think it these criminal proceeds never touch good people, or innocent families, or unemployed men and women just looking for a day's work.

But they do.

It doesn't take long before the billions generated from the sale of Afghan heroin seep into the broader fabric of everyday society. Heroin has brought prosperity to thousands of ordinary citizens in Afghanistan, and it has made millionaires out of tribal chiefs and warlords. And if the choice is between prosperity—delivered and sustained by criminal organizations—and poverty, it's no choice at all.

Drug Money and Corruption

But here is the dilemma, and it is a very serious one . . .

Countries become addicted to drug economies the same way people become addicted to drugs. That addiction—of people, institutions, and culture—to drug-dollars, is a real and immediate danger in Afghanistan. Indeed, even legitimate income flowing into the treasury of the new government, tax revenues, for example, comes from the import of luxury items: cars, trucks, consumer goods, purchased with drug profits.

In Afghanistan, or anyplace where drug money fuels the economy, drug dollars invariably make their way into the corridors of power as payoffs to government officials, bribes to courts and prosecutors, and as election funding for "drug-candidates," traffickers who run for office and win. There's also a brisk trade in "drugs for guns," a global, 24/7 exchange we know fuels terrorism and violence around the world.

What chance does democracy have in this environment? None.

How can the Rule of Law prevail? It cannot.

Legalizing drugs could make the current situation even worse.

Tough Remedies

Last week [January 2005] I was in Afghanistan to talk to President [Hamid] Karzai and members of his administration. I encouraged him to take tough measures against drug traffickers, and to support "a negative pledge"—a commitment by farmers to refrain from drug cultivation, as a condition for the receipt of grants, loans, and other development assistance. If eradication efforts do not materialize, monies from donor states, NGOs [non-governmental organizations], and other multilateral agencies would be rescinded.

The world needs to see results in Afghanistan, counternarcotic efforts that prove this fledgling democracy can, in fact, deliver on its promise to eradicate Afghanistan's poppy fields. I have also urged the Government of Afghanistan, and partner states threatened by an increasing influx of heroin, to respond to this challenge by offering one another mutual legal assistance and creating legal mechanisms to support the prosecution of drug traffickers. This may involve the issuance of international arrest warrants, a very bold, but necessary action.

We also talked about the need for judicial reform in Afghanistan. European States and other nations willing and able to extradite traffickers for trial in other countries need to help investigators and prosecutors in Afghanistan build strong cases that will hold up in any court. Without a strong and effective judiciary, drug traffickers and their dirty dollars will continue to do what they do best—buy police chiefs and judges, intimidate witnesses, and fund start-up enterprises like brothels filled with the victims of human trafficking—for the most part, women and children who are sexually exploited and left to die from HIV/AIDS. . . .

Legalization Is Not the Solution

Some people argue that drug legalization would change all this. It's a myth that won't disappear. Supporters call legalization a "realistic approach." *I call it wishful thinking.* The fact is that as bad as the drug situation is today, these are not "the worst of times" as regards the cultivation and trafficking of illegal drugs.

Today, the infamous Golden Triangle [the area where Myanmar, Laos, and Thailand meet] is virtually drug free. Coca cultivation has decreased dramatically in Colombia and the Andean region. And here's more positive news: in 2005, we expect only a marginal increase in the supply of opium worldwide, the result of a significant decline in Myanmar and Laos.

The history of drug cultivation and production also holds a lesson for critics who think drug control is an impossible dream. The problem we face today pales compared to the amount of opium coming out of India and China at the beginning of the 20th century. In the early 20th century, 50 million people were addicted to heroin in China.

In 2005, there are 15 million users.

One hundred years ago, global opium production had risen in India and China to an astonishing 30,000 tonnes, following its de facto legalization in China.

In 2005, the global production of opium, licit and illicit, amounts to only 5,000 tonnes.

A century ago, 80 million hectares were under cultivation in China—dedicated to opium.

In 2005, even factoring Afghanistan into the picture, less than 150,000 hectares are dedicated to the cultivation of poppies.

This decline, this progress, did not occur by accident.

It reflects serious, real-world efforts to eliminate drug cultivation and production. And it proves, beyond a doubt, that governments with the political will, strong legislation, and effective law enforcement and economic development policies can tackle this enormous problem—and solve it.

I wish I could convince the sceptics of that. Because none of these remedies will work without a commensurate shift in public attitude. Governments and their citizens must be of the collective opinion that drug production and drug use cannot be tolerated or accommodated. Without that consensus, we simply cannot win.

Here's another myth—that legalizing drugs will eliminate organized crime.

Organized crime did not disappear when Prohibition ended in the 20's in the United States; it simply diversified, moving resources and capital into other criminal sidelines. Indeed, legalizing drugs could make the current situation even worse.

Drug prices in consumer countries would go down. The consumption of increasing amounts of drugs would rise. And here's some information for the economists in this audience—I hope I'm not the only one: studies have shown that price elasticities for heroin and cocaine amount to a round -0.7 or more—which means a reduction in price of 10 percent would increase consumption by at least 7 percent.

Following legalization, prices in consumer countries would fall by more than 90 percent. The result? A zero decrease in organized crime, and a huge increase in the number of addicts worldwide. . . .

Organized Crime and Diversification

Organized Crime is always on the lookout for new opportunities—and war, or regional conflict, is one of the best. War provides almost unlimited occasions for illicit enrichment via profitable new trading deals. Insurgents can plunder a region's natural resources and trade these resources for weapons. In conflict zones, criminal networks routinely operate as intermediaries between legitimate businesses and black market operators.

Organized Crime was involved in the trafficking of light arms during the Balkan Civil War, arms which were reexported to Liberia and the Ivory Cost. And there are reports that these same arms are now finding their way to Sudan and east Congo.

Light arms trafficking, in particular, has led to a dramatic increase in casualties in war-torn regions and states, and to criminal violence afterwards. This is something that needs to be considered by lawmakers in countries that have not yet ratified the UN [United Nations] Protocol against Firearms.

Criminal organizations working with insurgents have also distributed drugs to child-soldiers, a technique used to turn these children into killing-machines. Ironically, the UN Office on Drugs and Crime is only able to reach these young victims after they have reached the age of adulthood. Still, in many cases, we are helping them cope with what often remains a lifetime addiction to drugs and violence.

Something else we often see during regional conflicts are "unholy alliances" between organized crime and local warlords. We see this today in Afghanistan, Colombia and Myanmar. Not too long ago, we saw the same thing in Guatemala, Peru, Bolivia, and Somalia. Local warlords—they're also called insurgents, commanders, guerrillas, or contras—always have an interest in blocking progress toward conflict resolution. For criminals and warlords, anarchy and lawlessness is *good* for business.

In post-conflict periods, when states try to focus on rebuilding and caring for citizens battered and displaced by war, criminal operators dig in for the long term. By this point, organized crime has become a major stakeholder in anarchy and lawlessness. Its goal is to maintain control of profitable turf, by nurturing discord, reopening old wounds, and undercutting the efforts of peacemakers.

Revenue from a supposedly 'harmless' drug like marijuana is enough to provide weapons to an entire army of child militias in Africa.

The Drug Connection

None of this, of course, would be possible without the annual guarantee of billions in drug revenues. Without these funds, undercapitalized, the criminal underworld would languish. The Rule of Law could take root in parts of the world where outlaws reign today. And for millions of people, in Africa, Asia, and in developing countries across the world, security, development and democracy might finally be within reach. . . .

Individuals tried for war crimes and found guilty must be jailed. The victims of regional conflicts, child soldiers, drug users and other populations scared by violence, must be rehabilitated and reintegrated into normal society. And drug users must be offered opportunities for rehabilitation.

None of this can happen until we admit the following: the victories of Organized Crime in failed states depend on revenue realized through drug trafficking.

The notion that a single good deed can cascade through society and change the lives of disparate beneficiaries is an old one. It reinforces the ancient human "hunch" that we are truly one family. It is impossible to believe that idea without also knowing, instinctively, that one evil inevitably flows from another and that every criminal act is likely father to another, perhaps more terrible, crime.

Let me end these remarks with the same claim I made at their beginning—drug dollars are the cash flow on which Organized Crime depends.

You may not see the connection between a single heroin buy on the streets of New York and the kidnapping in Southeast Asia and trafficking of a child for purposes of sexual exploitation, but it's there.

You may not understand the relationship between a warlord's greed in Afghanistan and a terrorist bombing in Western Europe, but it's real.

And you may not realize that revenue from a supposedly "harmless" drug like marijuana is enough to provide weapons to an entire army of child militias in Africa, but the connection exists.

It is our job, yours and mine, not to be "practical" about drugs and satisfied with halfway solutions, but to be passionate in our opposition to drug trafficking and determined, once and for all, to end it.

Islamic Terrorist Groups Use Heroin to Finance Their Terrorism

Josh Lefkowitz and Erick Stakelbeck

Josh Lefkowitz and Erick Stakelbeck are affiliated with the Investigative Project, a counterterrorism research institute.

An eye-opening report issued by the United Nations [UN] earlier this month [September 2004] revealed that every Al-Qaeda-linked terrorist attack to date—with the exception of 9/11—has cost under $50,000 to carry out.

Much of these funds, according to the report, "have been collected locally, whether through crime or diverted from charitable donations."

The numerous closures of Muslim "charities" in the U.S. since 9/11, including the recently-indicted Holy Land Foundation (which allegedly raised money for Hamas), in large part verify the UN's assessment.

But what about Al-Qaeda's links to international crime, in particular, the drug trade?

Al-Qaeda and the Drug Trade

A recent staff report released by the 9/11 Commission stated that "no substantial evidence" had been found that Al-Qaeda has played a major role in the drug trade, either before or after 9/11.

But from Southeast Asia to Western Europe, the opposite is true, as Al-Qaeda is using illegal drug money to help finance devastating attacks like last March's [2004] Madrid train bombings.

Josh Lefkowitz and Erick Stakelbeck, "Bin Laden's Hustlers," *FrontPageMagazine.com*, September 21, 2004. Reproduced by permission.

The epicenter for much of this Al-Qaeda drug activity is Afghanistan, where poppy cultivation has risen sharply since the overthrow of the Taliban in 2001. The poppy is converted into opium and heroin by criminal gangs, who then smuggle it out of Afghanistan and to the West (95 percent of the heroin in Britain, for instance, derives from Afghani opium).

Al-Qaeda works closely with these Afghan drug smugglers to secure safe routes for their shipments through neighboring Pakistan and Iran. But Al-Qaeda's assistance comes with a price: the group places heavy taxes on the shipments, and often takes some of the drugs as payment, using them later to buy weapons.

For the terrorists, drug trafficking serves as a lucrative means to further their jihad against the West.

Tactics similar to these were employed by the Madrid bombers, who, Spanish authorities believe, used 30 kilos of hashish to buy explosives that were used in that attack (which killed 200 people and wounded over a thousand more).

The men were also suspected of having links to Morocco's thriving hashish trade, which serves as a source of revenue for Islamic terrorists in North Africa and Europe.

But even prior to Madrid, a pair of discoveries by the U.S. Navy in December 2003 underscored Al-Qaeda's increased involvement in the drug business.

In one of those incidents, the U.S.S. *Decatur* intercepted a ship in the Persian Gulf that contained two tons of hashish worth between $8 and $10 million. Intelligence gained from this raid led the Navy to two other ships in the area, which were both loaded with methamphetamines and heroin.

In total, ten people arrested during these operations had Al-Qaeda ties.

Likewise, just two weeks later, while conducting a routine search of a small fishing boat in the Arabian Sea, a U.S. Navy vessel found several Al-Qaeda members huddled around a large stash of narcotics.

Other Terrorist Groups

Yet Al-Qaeda is not the only terrorist organization active in the drug trade. Both Jemaah Islamiyah, an Al-Qaeda-funded group based in Southeast Asia, and Hizb-i-Islami, which operates in and around Afghanistan, are known to deal in narcotics as well.

In addition, the Shiite group Hezbollah has long engaged in drugs-for-cash deals, with operatives smuggling cocaine from Latin America (often by way of the notorious "tri-border" region, where Brazil, Paraguay and Argentina meet) to Europe and the Middle East.

In the past, Hezbollah has also smuggled opiates out of Lebanon's Bekaa Valley, a lawless area that is a haven for drug smugglers and Islamic terrorists. The increased cooperation between these two factions seems contradictory at first glance, given Islam's historically strong opposition to drug use. But for the terrorists, drug trafficking serves as a lucrative means to further their jihad [holy war] against the West.

As a U.S. defense official told the *Washington Times*: "Bin Laden does not mind trafficking in drugs, even though it's against the teaching of Islam, because it's being used to kill Westerners."

It's clear that terror groups tied to the drug trade are reaping the benefits. Taliban remnants in Afghanistan, for example, are reportedly spending millions of dollars per month to plan attacks that would disrupt that country's upcoming elections.

And over the past several months, during raids on Al-Qaeda safe houses in Saudi Arabia, Saudi security forces have seized close to a billion dollars worth of cash, weapons and equipment. It's no secret that Al-Qaeda elements in the Kingdom have close ties with drug smugglers in Yemen and Afghanistan.

Gen. Richard B. Myers, chairman of the Joint Chiefs of Staff, recently admitted that there was growing concern amongst American officials concerning the drugs-and-terror link, and said that the U.S. is working on a strategy to combat Al-Qaeda's involvement in the narcotics trade.

Until that plan is devised, however, cutting off the increasingly creative sources of funding for Al-Qaeda and its ilk will remain one of the more complex—and crucial—challenges in the War on Terror.

Outlawing Drug Trafficking Helps to Support Terrorists

Ted Galen Carpenter

Ted Galen Carpenter is the vice president for defense and foreign policy studies at the Cato Institute.

Under pressure from Washington, Afghan President Hamid Karzai is urging his people to fight narcotics as ferociously as they fought the Soviet occupation in the 1980s. Such a struggle seems destined to undermine the campaign against al-Qaeda and the Taliban. Karzai and his American patrons can prevail against the country's opium growers or its terrorists, but not both.

Afghanistan has been one of the leading sources of opium poppies, and therefore heroin, since the 1970s. Today [January 2005], the country accounts for more than 75% of the world's opium supply. It is clear that some of the revenues from the drug trade—at least 10% to 20%—flow into the coffers of al-Qaeda and the Taliban.

That is obviously a worrisome development. But it is hardly unprecedented. For years, leftist insurgent groups in Colombia, principally the Revolutionary Armed Forces of Colombia (FARC), and right-wing paramilitaries have been financed largely by that country's cocaine trade. Conservative estimates place the annual revenue stream to the FARC alone at between US$515 million and US$600 million per year. (In 2002, the U.S. ambassador to Colombia put the figure at "several billion" dollars.)

The harsh reality is that terrorist groups around the world have been enriched by prohibitionist drug policies that drive up drug costs, and which deliver enormous profits to the outlaw organizations willing to accept the risks that go with the trade.

Targeting the Afghanistan drug trade would create a variety of problems. Most of the regional warlords who abandoned the Taliban and currently support the U.S. anti-terror campaign (and in many cases politically undergird the Karzai government) are deeply involved in the drug trade, in part to pay the militias that give them political clout. A crusade against drug trafficking could easily alienate those regional power brokers and cause them to switch allegiances yet again.

Drug prohibition is terrorism's best friend.

Unfortunately, Washington is now increasing its pressure on the Karzai government to crack down on opium cultivation, offering more than a billion dollars in aid to fund anti-drug efforts. In addition, Secretary of Defence Donald Rumsfeld announced in August [2004] that U.S. military forces in Afghanistan would make drug eradication a high priority—a mission that the military properly continues to resist.

Terrorism Is Worse than Drugs

U.S. officials need to keep their goals straight. Recognizing that security considerations sometimes trump other objectives would not be an unprecedented move by Washington. U.S. agencies quietly ignored the drug-trafficking activities of anti-communist factions in Central America during the 1980s when the primary goal was to keep those countries out of the Soviet orbit. In the early 1990s, the United States also eased its pressure on Peru's government to eradicate drugs when President Alberto Fujimori concluded that a higher priority had to be given to winning coca farmers away from Shining Path guerrillas. U.S. leaders should refrain from trying to make U.S. soldiers into anti-drug crusaders: Even those policymakers who support the war on drugs as an overall policy ought to recognize that American troops in Central Asia have a difficult enough job fighting terrorists.

There is little doubt that terrorist groups around the world profit from the drug trade. What anti-drug crusaders refuse to acknowledge, however, is that the connection between drug trafficking and terrorism is the direct result of making drugs illegal. The prohibitionist policy that the United States and other drug-consuming countries continue to pursue guarantees a huge black market premium for all illegal drugs. The retail value of drugs coming into the United States (to say nothing of Europe and other markets) is estimated at US$50 billion to US$100 billion a year. Fully 90% of that sum is attributable to the prohibition premium.

Absent a world-wide prohibitionist policy, this fat profit margin would evaporate, and terrorist organizations would be forced to seek other sources of revenue.

Drug prohibition is terrorism's best friend. That symbiotic relationship will continue until the United States and its allies have the wisdom to dramatically change their drug policies.

Legalizing Heroin Would Stifle Black Market Trade and Terrorists' Profits

Scott McPherson

Scott McPherson is a contributor to many publications, including Freedom Daily, Liberty, *and* CNSNews.com.

Government officials find it difficult to admit when they're wrong. Perhaps, like people in general, they see such an admission as a sign of weakness, and prefer to rationalize their failure rather than change their approach. This inevitably leads to calls for a "strengthening" of current policy and an expansion of the program in question.

The war on drugs is a perfect example. The U.S. government has been fighting intensely to rid the country of "dangerous drugs" for about 40 years now—much longer, some would argue—and year after year the war's failures mount.

We citizens are regularly assured that the "tide is turning," usually after some recent antidrug operation has yielded the "largest ever" bust in history, and thus we must "stay the course" in our antidrug efforts. Somehow the drug warriors never seem to realize that "largest ever" is an admission of failure. How can we possibly be winning this war if larger and larger shipments of drugs are being smuggled across our borders?

Americans are using drugs today just as they were last year, and the year before that, and the year before that, fueling the demand that keeps dealers in business—despite the desperate attempts of the United States and other governments to stifle drug production and exportation around the world. On Aug. 24, 2006, Agence France-Presse [AFP] reported that the

Scott McPherson, "Fight Terrorism: Legalize Heroin," *Liberty*, vol. 21, January, 2007. Reproduced by permission.

British government, which is now in charge of antidrug operations in Afghanistan, "is aiming for a 70 percent reduction in the next five years and elimination within 10 years" of Afghanistan's opium trade. Governments just love those Five-Year Plans.

Why this sense of urgency? According to an Associated Press [AP] report in the Sept. 3 *New Hampshire Union-Leader*, "Afghanistan's world-leading opium cultivation rose a 'staggering' 60 percent this year, the UN [United Nations] anti-drugs chief announced." *Sixty percent!*

Eradicating Opium

For years, Republicans have been talking up the need to reduce opium production in Afghanistan. House Speaker Dennis Hastert said in 2001 that "the illegal drug trade is the financial engine that fuels many terrorist organizations around the world, including Osama Bin Laden," and in October 2003, the *Washington Times* reported that "the [President George W.] Bush administration has talked publicly of ridding Afghanistan of its lucrative poppy crop that provides 70 percent of the world's heroin." "Ridding" is an unequivocal term—like "largest ever."

Obviously things haven't turned out quite the way those in charge planned. A June 7 [2006] article on the Radio Free Europe/Radio Liberty website reported that Afghanistan's southern Helmand Province is expected to yield a "bumper crop" of opium this year [2007]. Ditto other parts of the country, pushing what was already the world's largest opium producer even higher up the ladder, to about 76% of world opium production. AFP claims that "Between 70 and 90 percent of heroin used in Europe originates in Afghanistan."

International efforts to control opium production in Afghanistan aren't failing from a lack of resolve. In early 2001 the United States government allocated $43 million in humanitarian aid to help wean opium growers off their cash crop. After Sept. 11, 2001, the American and European governments seized an estimated $24 million in assets linked to al Qaeda, which is widely believed to fund its activities through opium and heroin sales.

Asking an Afghan peasant to give up poppy growing would be like asking a dairy farmer to surrender his cows.

Today NATO [North Atlantic Treaty Organization] troops occupy the country—a strategic scenario that U.S. drug warriors can only salivate at replicating stateside—and Afghan President Hamid Karzai has a firm antiopium policy, creating a Counternarcotics Ministry in his government and outdoing the rest of the world by declaring not just a war but a "holy war" on narcotics. Congress earmarked $774 million for antinarcotics activities in Afghanistan in 2005, and allocated another $510 million for 2006–2007.

Alongside U.S. and NATO efforts are those of the British, with the Labour government's antidrug minister, Bill Rammel, promising a "dismantling" of the "opium economy." In his shadow lies waiting the Conservative opposition minister, who, employing the "me too" line of attack typical of opportunistic politicians, has criticized Labour's efforts as insufficient "with the level of forces [in Afghanistan] that we've got."

The full force of many governments is unmistakably behind this endeavor, with even more resources promised. Despite this, the AP reported (Sept. 3 [2006]) that opium production is actually "outstripping the demand of the world's heroin users by a third." The U.S. Department fears that Afghanistan is becoming a "narcotics state."

All of which could lead a discerning individual to a three-fold conclusion: opium growing on net is unaffected by eradication efforts, heroin demand around the world is on the rise (the UN Office of Drugs and Crime reports an increase in addiction in Central Asia, Russia, and Eastern Europe), and producers are not the least bit afraid of the international antidrug movement.

Afghanistan's Future

None of this bodes well for the future of Afghanistan, or the war on drugs. The U.S. government launched military operations against the Taliban immediately after the terrorist attacks of Sept. 11, 2001, installing a government friendly to the United States and hostile to terrorist groups like al Qaeda that are believed to traffic in narcotics to fund their attacks. Sadly, the U.S. government didn't take into account certain conditions that would undermine its objectives. For example, the opium trade makes up between 35% and 50% of the economy in Afghanistan, "where gross income [from heroin sales] was around 1.2 billion dollars last year" (AFP). Asking an Afghan peasant to give up poppy growing would be like asking a dairy farmer to surrender his cows.

Afghan farmers grow opium because increasing numbers of Americans, Canadians, Europeans, and Asians want to use heroin.

Add to this the fact that Taliban and al Qaeda forces still operating in the hinterlands of the Wild Wild East are in a position, irrespective of the western military presence, to demand and reward loyalty from local farmers. It's no surprise, then, that there's a ready supply of opium growers with no love for those who would take away their livelihood, preferring instead those who spend their profits killing westerners. Not exactly a promising set of circumstances.

Most important, however, is the economics of drug dealing itself. Legislators and military strategists may decree what they like, but the laws of supply and demand cannot be ignored for long: Afghan farmers grow opium because increasing, numbers of Americans, Canadians, Europeans, and Asians want to use heroin. This demand drives supply, providing every incentive for those who grow opium to continue doing so. Any short-term "success" in limiting supply—such as the UN's claim that its policies have reduced the amount of land under opium cultivation by 21%—will only backfire in the long term: all things remaining equal, any reduction in supply merely drives up prices, boosting profits and creating incentives to expand the trade. Hence a 60% increase in opium cultivation despite years of effort to reverse the trend—and more money for the terrorists.

With stubbornness characteristic of government officials, Antonio Maria Costa, the UN's version of a drug czar, wants to "crack down" on Afghan opium farming. What exactly does he think has been going on for the last five years?

One Five-Year Plan begets another, ensuring another half-decade of failed policies and another billion-plus dollars down the drain. And the same flawed logic that views "largest ever" seizures of drugs as a signal of drug war success is apparently prompting U.S., UN, and NATO leaders to see a spike in opium production, heroin sales, and heroin addiction as a sign to "stay the course" in the fight for eradication—no doubt with expanded wherewithal and renewed determination. This is all sounding very familiar.

Antiopium laws only drive a wedge between Afghan citizens and their government that can easily be exploited by people with murderous designs.

Legalizing Heroin

A wiser course would be to take the profits from heroin sales out of the pockets of terrorists through legalization. Though long the dream of "kooky" libertarians, this idea might be edging its way into the mainstream. Emmanuel Reinert, executive director of the Senlis Council, an international policy thinktank with offices in Kabul, London, Paris, and Brussels, told Radio Free Europe/Radio Liberty (June [2006]) that: "[Legalization] would be a way for the central government [of Afghanistan] to collaborate with local communities, and not to alienate them or antagonize them, as is currently the case with the eradication policy."

Further, he said that such a move would "develop sustainable economic activities for Afghanistan, but on top of that you will bring the rule of law and good governance in the provinces."

Anyone familiar with the war on drugs in the United States can see the wisdom in Reinert's words. Making something in high demand illegal merely drives the production and sale of that particular item into the hands of black-marketeers, thus undermining the rule of law. Quite the contrary of "good governance," prohibition puts the government in the position of harassing, intimidating, and ultimately bringing the full force of the law to bear against people who are merely satisfying the demand of willing buyers.

In Afghanistan this alienates and antagonizes those communities that make their living from growing poppies and, by encouraging people to thwart the taw, makes a mockery of the law and turns government into a bully that destroys their livelihood. Antiopium laws only drive a wedge between Afghan citizens and their government that can easily be exploited by people with murderous designs.

Legalization would surely end all that, and turn an outlawed practice into a "sustainable economic activity" with considerable benefits. The 21st Amendment repealed the prohibition on alcohol in the United States, and took alcohol production, sales, and distribution (and profits from same) out of the hands of organized crime bosses and put it in the hands of free-market businessmen. It also led to improved quality and a lower risk of alcohol poisoning.

If opium production were legalized, pharmaceutical companies rather than al Qaeda terrorists would be running the opium show in the Helmand Province, creating booming local economies and raising the living standards of Afghan peasants. Then Bayer or Dowpharma or Sandoz rather than Osama bin Laden would be profiting from the $11 billion Americans spend on heroin each year. Note that none of those companies currently sells heroin, and terrorists don't manufacture headache tablets, despite the enormous profit potential in both businesses.

With the government working alongside international pharmaceutical giants, the agricultural economy would be protected, and very likely expand, offering more jobs to locals. Instead of arresting local officials, spraying poppy fields with dangerous chemicals, and sending Special Forces operatives to kick down doors, a collaborative, mutually beneficial relationship could be developed between poor peasants and the new government in Kabul [the capital of Afghanistan] that would undermine al Qaeda and Taliban insurgents.

Stubborn Governments

The worst thing that could happen to narcoterrorists is legalization of their trade. Unfortunately, there's no reason to expect a much-needed radical shift in policy. The United Nations blames heavy rainfall for the spike in opium production; Karzai blames a lack of support from western governments; Britain's opposition Conservative Party blames low troop levels; and the U.S. government blames Karzai.

Legalization is the last thing on their minds. Just as there is big money for terrorists in the drug trade, there is big money, power, and prestige for government officials in continuing to fight this unwinnable war on drugs. While they rationalize failures, point fingers, call for more funding, and declare yet another "crackdown," the poppies are in full bloom and terrorists are using the profits to plan murders.

A common definition of insanity is repeating the same mistake over and over again, all the while expecting different results. The international war on drugs is a perfect example. World leaders are right to see legalization as an admission of failure, but admitting one is wrong and learning from a mistake is a signal of strength and good sense, not weakness.

Drug war opponents have long noted that prohibition undermines the rule of law, encourages the corruption of government officials, tears at the social fabric, strains relations between police and citizenry, destroys communities, and emboldens the criminal element. These costs are already high enough. Add to them the additional consequence of enriching terrorists, and we have the crowning reason to legalize opium manufacturing in Afghanistan and heroin around the world.

The United States Should Encourage Legal Opiate Production in Afghanistan

Anne Applebaum

Anne Applebaum is an author and a columnist for the Washington Post *and* Slate. *Her book* Gulag: A History *won the 2004 Pulitzer Prize.*

The British Empire once fought a war for the right to sell opium in China.

In retrospect, history has judged that war destructive and wasteful, a shameless battle of colonizers against colonized that in the end helped neither side.

Now NATO [North Atlantic Treaty Organization] is fighting a war to eradicate opium from Afghanistan. Allegedly, this time around the goals are different. According to the modern British government, Afghanistan's illicit-drug trade poses the "gravest threat to the long term security, development and effective governance of Afghanistan," particularly since the Taliban are believed to be the biggest beneficiaries of drug sales. Convinced that this time they are doing the morally right thing, Western governments are spending hundreds of millions of dollars bulldozing poppy fields, building up counternarcotics squads, and financing alternative crops in Afghanistan. Chemical spraying may begin as early as this spring [2007]. But, in retrospect, might history not judge this war to be every bit as destructive and wasteful as the original Opium Wars?

Fighting Opium Is Futile

Of course, right now it isn't fashionable to argue for any legal form of opiate cultivation. But look at the evidence. At the moment, Afghanistan's opium exports account for somewhere between two-thirds and one-third of the country's GDP [gross domestic product], depending on whether you believe the United Nations [U.N.] or the United States. The biggest producers are in the southern provinces where the Taliban is at its strongest. Every time a poppy field is destroyed, a poor person becomes poorer—and more likely to support the Taliban against the Western forces who wrecked his crops. Every time money is spent on alternative crops, it has to be distributed through a corrupt or nonexistent local bureaucracy. To date, the results of all this are utterly dispiriting. According to a U.S. government report from December 2006, the amount of land dedicated to poppy production *grew* last year [2006] by more than 60 percent. So central is the problem that Afghan President Hamid Karzai has called opium a "cancer" worse than terrorism. Spraying may make things worse: Not only will it cause environmental and health damage, Western planes dropping poisonous chemicals from the sky will feel to the local population like a military attack.

The best way to "ensure more Western soldiers get killed" is to expand poppy eradication further.

Yet by far the most depressing aspect of the Afghan poppy crisis is the fact that it exists at all—because it doesn't have to. To see what I mean, look at the history of Turkey, where once upon a time the drug trade also threatened the country's political and economic stability. Just like Afghanistan, Turkey had a long tradition of poppy cultivation. Just like Afghanistan, Turkey worried that poppy eradication could bring down the government. Just like Afghanistan, Turkey—this was the era of *Midnight Express*—was identified as the main source of the heroin sold in the West. Just like in Afghanistan, a ban was tried, and it failed.

As a result, in 1974, the Turks, with U.S. and U.N. support, tried a different tactic. They began licensing poppy cultivation for the purpose of producing morphine, codeine, and other legal opiates. Legal factories were built to replace the illegal ones. Farmers registered to grow poppies, and they paid taxes. You wouldn't necessarily know this from the latest White House drug strategy report—which devotes several pages to Afghanistan but doesn't mention Turkey—but the U.S. government still supports the Turkish program, even requiring U.S. drug companies to purchase 80 percent of what the legal documents euphemistically refer to as "narcotic raw materials" from the two traditional producers, Turkey and India.

A Better Way

Why not add Afghanistan to this list? The only good arguments against doing so—as opposed to the silly, politically correct, "just say no" arguments—are technical: that the weak or nonexistent bureaucracy will be no better at licensing poppy fields than at destroying them, or that some of the raw material will still fall into the hands of the drug cartels. Yet some of these problems can be solved by building processing factories at the local level and working within local power structures. And even if the program only succeeds in stopping half the drug trade, then a huge chunk of Afghanistan's economy will still emerge from the gray market, the power of the drug barons will be reduced, and, most of all, Western money will have been visibly spent helping Afghan farmers survive instead of destroying their livelihoods. The director of the Senlis Council, a group that studies the drug problem in Afghanistan, told me he reckons that the best way to "ensure more Western soldiers get killed" is to expand poppy eradication further.

Besides, things really could get worse. It isn't so hard to imagine, two or three years down the line, yet another emergency presidential speech calling for yet another "surge" of troops—but this time to southern Afghanistan, where impoverished villagers, having turned against the West, are joining the Taliban in droves. Before we get there, maybe it's worth letting some legal poppies bloom.

Organizations to Contact

The editors have compiled the following list of organizations concerned with the issues debated in this book. The descriptions are derived from materials provided by the organizations. All have publications or information available for interested readers. The list was compiled on the date of publication of the present volume; the information provided here may change. Be aware that many organizations take several weeks or longer to respond to inquiries, so allow as much time as possible.

American Civil Liberties Union (ACLU)
125 Broad St., Eighteenth Floor, New York, NY   10004
(212) 549-2500 • fax: (212) 549-2646
e-mail: aclu@aclu.org
Web site: www.aclu.org

The ACLU is a national organization that defends Americans' civil rights as guaranteed in the U.S. Constitution. It operates the Drug Law Reform Project, which provides legal assistance to people whose constitutional and human rights have been infringed by the war on drugs. The ACLU's publications include the report *Caught in the Net: The Impact of Drug Policies on Women and Families* and the position paper "Race and the War on Drugs."

Cato Institute
1000 Massachusetts Ave. NW, Washington, DC   20001
(202) 842-0200 • fax: (202) 842-3490
Web site: www.cato.org

The Cato Institute is a public policy research foundation dedicated to limiting the power of government and to protecting individual liberty. The institute strongly opposes the war on drugs and its effects on individual freedoms. Cato publishes the *Cato Journal* three times per year and the *Cato Policy Report* bimonthly. It also publishes numerous white papers and briefings, including "Treating Doctors as Drug Dealers: The DEA's War on Prescription Painkillers," "Two Restrained Cheers for Mexico's New Drug Law," and "The Drug War Toll Mounts."

Drug Enforcement Administration (DEA)

2401 Jefferson Davis Highway, Alexandria, VA   22301
Web site: www.usdoj.gov/dea

The DEA is the federal agency charged with enforcing the nation's drug laws. The agency concentrates on stopping the smuggling and distribution of narcotics in the United States and abroad. It publishes *Drug Enforcement Magazine* three times a year.

Drug Free America Foundation

2600 Ninth St. Suite 200, St. Petersburg, FL   33704
(727) 828-0211 • fax: (727) 828-0212
Web site: www.dfaf.org

The Drug Free America Foundation is not-for-profit organization committed to developing, promoting, and sustaining global strategies, policies, and laws that will reduce illegal drug use, drug addiction, drug-related injury, and death. The foundation opposes legalizing drugs and supports government efforts to intercept shipments of drugs. The foundation publishes a biweekly newsletter, as well as videos and publications for teenagers and parents about the dangers of drug use.

Drug Policy Alliance (DPA)

70 West Thirty-sixth St., Sixteenth Floor
New York, NY   10018
(212) 613-8020 • fax: (212) 613-8021
e-mail: nyc@drugpolicy.org
Web site: www.drugpolicy.org

The DPA was formed by the 2000 merger of two other drug-policy organizations, the Lindesmith Center and the Drug Policy Foundation. The DPA advocates for decriminalizing marijuana, ending mandatory minimum sentences for non-violent drug offenders, and increasing support for drug-treatment and harm-reduction programs. Its publications include *Disparity by Design: How Drug-Free Zone Laws Impact Racial Disparity—and Fail to Protect Youth* and the *Drug Policy Reform Congressional Voter Guide.*

Drug Reform Coordination Network (DRCNet)
1623 Connecticut Ave. NW, Third Floor
Washington, DC   20009
(202) 293-8340 • fax: (202) 293-8344
e-mail: drcnet@drcnet.org
Web site: http://stopthedrugwar.org

DRCNet is an educational and advocacy organization that supports a less restrictive drug policy. DRCNet believes that the sale and use of drugs should be legalized and legally regulated rather than banned. DRCNet publishes *Drug War Chronicle* (a weekly online newsletter) as well as several blogs dealing with drug-related issues.

Hoover Institution On War, Revolution and Peace
434 Galvez Mall, Stanford University, Stanford, CA   94305
(650) 723-1754 • fax: (650) 723-1687
Web site: www.hoover.org

The Hoover Institution on War, Revolution and Peace at Stanford University is a conservative public policy research center devoted to advanced study of politics, economics, and international affairs. The institution's researchers believe that the war on drugs endangers Americans' freedoms and interferes with efforts to fight terrorism. The Hoover Institution's many periodical publications include *Weekly Essays, Hoover Digest, and Policy Review.* The Hoover Institution also publishes books, including *Drug War Deadlock: The Policy Battle Continues.*

Latin American Working Group (LAWG)
110 Maryland Ave. NE, Box 15, Washington, DC   20002
(202) 546-7010
Web site: www.lawg.org

LAWG advocates for U.S. policies toward Latin America that promote human rights, justice, peace, and sustainable development. It opposes antidrug measures that threaten human rights, particularly the use of the military to fight drug trafficking. Its publications include the reports *Going to Extremes: The Aerial Spraying Program in Colombia and Troubling Patterns: The Mexican Military and the War on Drugs*, as well as the newsletter *Advocate.*

National Center on Addiction and Substance Abuse at Columbia University (CASA)
633 Third Ave., Nineteenth Floor, New York, NY   10017
(212) 841-5200 • fax: (212) 956-8020
Web site: www.casacolumbia.org

CASA is a private nonprofit organization that works to educate the public about the costs and hazards of substance abuse and that researches best practices in prevention, treatment, and law enforcement. The center supports treatment as the best way to reduce drug addiction. Its publications include *CASA Inside Newsletter*, which is published three times per year; the book *High Society: How Substance Abuse Ravages America and What to Do About It*; and the report *"You've Got Drugs!": Prescription Drug Pushers on the Internet.*

National Clearinghouse for Alcohol and Drug Information
PO Box 2345, Rockville, MD   20847
(800) 729-6686 • fax: (301) 468-6433
Web site: http://ncadi.samhsa.gov

The National Clearinghouse for Alcohol and Drug Information distributes publications of the U.S. Department of Health and Human Services, the National Institute on Drug Abuse, and other federal agencies concerned with alcohol and drug abuse. Publications distributed through the clearinghouse include a variety of brochures, videos, posters, and other items dealing with all types of drugs.

National Institute on Drug Abuse (NIDA)
6001 Executive Blvd., Room 5213, Bethesda, MD   20892
(301) 443-1124
e-mail: information@nida.nih.gov
Web site: www.drugabuse.gov

NIDA is a government agency that supports and conducts research on drug abuse to improve addiction prevention, treatment, and policy efforts. It publishes the yearly *Monitoring the Future Survey*, the bimonthly *NIDA Notes* newsletter, and a number of fact sheets and research reports.

National Organization for the Reform of Marijuana Laws (NORML)
1600 K St. NW, Suite 501, Washington, DC   20006
(202) 483-5500 • fax: (202) 483-0057
e-mail: norml@norml.org
Web site: www.norml.org

NORML fights to legalize marijuana and to help those who have been convicted and sentenced for possessing or selling marijuana. Its publications include "Rethinking the Consequences of Decriminalizing Marijuana" and *Crimes of Indiscretion: Marijuana Arrests in the United States.*

November Coalition
282 West Astor, Colville, WA   99114
(509) 684-1550
e-mail: moreinfo@november.org
Web site: www.november.org

The November Coalition is a not-for-profit organization that was founded in 1997 to educate the public about the increasing number of people being jailed on drug charges and about the destructive consequences of those incarcerations. The coalition advocates for an end to prisoner abuse, for sentencing reform, and for an end to police reliance on other criminals as informants in drug cases. The coalition publishes the *Razor Wire* newsletter.

RAND Corporation

PO Box 2138, Santa Monica, CA   90407
(310) 393-0411 • fax: (310) 393-4818
Web site: www.rand.org

RAND is a nonpartisan, nonprofit organization that seeks to improve policy and decisionmaking through research and analysis. RAND's Drug Policy Research Center conducts research on such topics as the results of decriminalizing marijuana, the effectiveness of mandatory minimum sentences for drug offenses, and the economics of drug dealing. Its extensive list of publications includes *How Goes the "War on Drugs"?: An Assessment of U.S. Drug Problems and Policy* and the monthly online newsletter *DPRC Insights*.

Reason Foundation

3415 S. Supulveda Blvd., Suite 400, Los Angeles, CA   90034
(310) 391-2245 • fax: (310) 391-4395
Web site: www.reason.org

This public policy organization researches contemporary social and political problems and promotes libertarian philosophy and free-market principles. It publishes the monthly *Reason* magazine and the Web site *Reason Online*, both of which contain articles and editorials criticizing the ways that the war on drugs infringes on Americans' civil liberties.

Senlis Council

17 Queen Anne's Gate, London   SW1H 9BU
  United Kingdom
+44 20 7222 2901 • fax: +44 20 7222 2927
Web site: www.senliscouncil.net

The Senlis Council is an international think tank that promotes innovative analysis and proposals in the areas of foreign policy, security, development, and counternarcotics policy. The council sponsors an extensive program in Afghanistan to investigate the relationships between counternarcotics, military, and development policies and their consequences on Afghanistan's reconstruction efforts. The council's publications include *Poppy for Medicine* and *Feasibility Study on Opium Licensing in Afghanistan*.

United Nations Office on Drugs and Crime (UNODC)
Vienna International Centre, PO Box 500, Vienna   A-1400
  Austria
+43 1 26060 0 • fax: +43 1 26060 5866
Web site: www.unodc.org

The UNODC was founded in 1997 to help United Nations member countries fight illegal drugs, crime, and terrorism. The UNODC performs research and analysis to help increase knowledge of issues related to drugs and crime and provides technical assistance to countries that want help fighting drugs, crime, and terrorism. Its publications include the annual *World Drug Report*, the journal *Bulletin on Narcotics*, and the quarterly magazine *Perspectives*.

White House Office of National Drug Control Policy (ONDCP)
Executive Office of the President, Washington, DC   20503
(800) 666-3332 • fax: (301) 519-5212
Web site: www.whitehousedrugpolicy.gov

The ONDCP is an agency within the executive branch of the federal government that establishes policies, priorities, and objectives for the U.S.'s antidrug programs. The ONDCP also helps to coordinate the antidrug efforts of other government agencies, including programs run by the U.S. State Department and by local governments. The ONDCP prepares and publishes the annual *President's National Drug Control Strategy* and numerous other documents relating to drug-control programs.

Bibliography

Books

Enrique Desmond Arias
: *Drugs and Democracy in Rio de Janeiro: Trafficking, Social Networks, and Public Security*. Chapel Hill: University of North Carolina Press, 2006.

Guy Arnold
: *The International Drugs Trade*. New York: Routledge, 2004.

David Boyum and Peter Reuter
: *An Analytic Assessment of U.S. Drug Policy*. Washington, DC: AEI Press, 2005.

Jonathan P. Caulkins, Peter H. Reuter, Martin Y. Iguchi, and James Chiesa
: *How Goes the "War on Drugs"? An Assessment of U.S. Drugs Problems and Policy*. Santa Monica, CA: RAND, 2005.

Frederick J. DesRoches
: *The Crime That Pays: Drug Trafficking and Organized Crime in Canada*. Toronto: Canadian Scholars' Press, 2005.

Laura E. Huggins, ed.
: *Drug War Deadlock: The Policy Battle Continues*. Stanford, CA: Hoover Institution Press, 2005.

Douglas N. Husak
: *Legalize This!: The Case for Decriminalizing Drugs*. New York: Verso, 2002.

Robin Kirk   *More Terrible than Death: Massacres, Drugs, and America's War in Colombia.* New York: Public Affairs, 2003.

Grace Livingstone   *Inside Colombia: Drugs, Democracy and War.* New Brunswick, New Jersey: Rutgers University Press, 2004.

David R. Mares   *Drug Wars and Coffeehouses: The Political Economy of the International Drug Trade.* Washington, DC: CQ Press, 2006.

Jeffrey A. Miron   *Drug War Crimes: The Consequences of Prohibition.* Oakland, CA: Independent Institute, 2004.

Matthew B.   *Lies, Damned Lies, and Drug War*
Robinson and   *Statistics: A Critical Analysis of Claims*
Renee G. Scherlen   *Made by the Office of National Drug Control Policy.* Albany: State University of New York Press, 2007.

Jacob Sullum   *Saying Yes: In Defense of Drug Use.* New York: Tarcher, 2003.

Albert Tavidze,   *Andean Regional Initiative.* New York:
ed.   Nova Science Publishers, 2004.

Kimberley L.   *Transnational Threats: Smuggling and*
Thachuk, ed.   *Trafficking in Arms, Drugs, and Human Life.* Westport, CT: Praeger Security International, 2007.

Francisco E.   *Illegal Drugs, Economy, and Society in*
Thoumi   *the Andes.* Washington, DC: Woodrow Wilson Center Press, 2003.

Periodicals

Scott Baldauf and Faye Bowers	"Afghanistan Riddled with Drug Ties," *Christian Science Monitor*, May 13, 2005.
Radley Balko	"The Case of Cory Maye: A Cop Is Dead, an Innocent Man May Be on Death Row, and Drug Warriors Keep Knocking Down Doors," *Reason*, October 2006.
Ted Galen Carpenter	"Washington's Unsavory Antidrug Partners," *USA Today Magazine*, November 2002.
Marc Chernick	"Just Say No: The War on Terror Will Fail Unless the United States Heeds the Lessons from Its Disastrous War on Drugs," *WorldLink*, July–August, 2002.
Tom Coghlan	"Smash Our Trade in Opium, Afghans Tell British," *Telegraph* (London), May 25, 2007.
Pamela Constable	"A Poor Yield for Afghans' War on Drugs," *Washington Post*, September 19, 2006.
Joseph Contreras	"Failed 'Plan': After Five Years and Billions of U.S. Aid in the Drug War, Cocaine Production Still Thrives," *Newsweek International*, August 29, 2005.
Joshua Davis	"The Mystery of the Coca Plant That Wouldn't Die," *Wired*, November 2004.

Economist	"Just Say Maybe," April 5, 2003.
Patrick Farrell	"Methamphetamine Fuels the West's Oil and Gas Boom," *High Country News*, October 3, 2005.
Danna Harman	"The War on Drugs: Ambushed in Jamundi," *Christian Science Monitor*, September 27, 2006.
Danna Harman	"Plan Colombia: Big Gains, but Cocaine Still Flows," *Christian Science Monitor*, September 28, 2006.
Danna Harman	"Rethinking Plan Colombia: Some Ways to Fix It," *Christian Science Monitor*, September 29, 2006.
Christopher Hitchens	"Let the Afghan Poppies Bloom," *Slate*, December 13, 2004.
Mary Jordan and Kevin Sullivan	"Border Police Chief Only Latest Casualty in Mexico Drug War," *Washington Post*, June 16, 2005.
Johnathan Last	"We Are Winning the War on Drugs," *Philadelphia Enquirer*, February 5, 2006.
Latin Trade	"Collateral Damage: The U.S. War on Drugs Keeps Latin America's Poor Farmers Tethered to the Trade," September 2003.
James C. McKinley Jr.	"With Beheadings and Attacks, Drug Gangs Terrorize Mexico," *New York Times*, October 26, 2006.

Josh Meyer   "Burdened U.S. Military Cuts Role in
                    Drug War," *Los Angeles Times*, Janu-
                    ary 22, 2007.

Margot Roosevelt   "The Cold-Pill Crackdown: To Fight
                    the Meth Epidemic, States Go After
                    Legal Sniffle Remedies at the Corner
                    Drugstore," *Time*, February 7, 2005.

David Rose   "The House of Death," *Observer*
                    (London), December 3, 2006.

Tina Rosenberg   "When Is a Pain Doctor a Drug
                    Pusher?," *New York Times Magazine*,
                    June 17, 2007.

Jim Schoettler   "Lure of 'The Game,'" *Jacksonville
                    (FL) Times-Union*, January 18, 2007.

Jason Trahan   "'Cheese' Using, Abusing Youths,"
                    Dallas Morning News, February 23,
                    2007.

Michelle Tsai   "How Much for All That Heroin?"
                    Slate, May 24, 2007.

Internet Source

Frank Smyth   "Bush's Brush with Latin America's
                    Drug Lords," *Nation*, March 9, 2007.
                    www.thenation.com/doc/20070326/
                    smyth.

Index

A

Addiction treatment programs, 38–39

Adolescents
  drug overdoses of, 37
  drug use of, 19–20, 26

Aerial fumigation. See Fumigation of crops

Afghanistan, 198–199
  antidrug efforts in, 210–211
  corruption and drug money in, 209–210
  drug trafficking in, 201–202, 216–219
  economy and drugs in, 208–209, 226
  invasion by Soviet Union, 199
  terrorism in, 201–202, 216–219
  See also Opium

African Americans
  crack cocaine and, 94–95, 103
  drug policy consequences for, 96
  framing of, 76
  imprisonment of, 42, 93, 95, 97
  prison time vs. college time, 95, 96

AIDS, 51, 207, 211

Air Bridge Denial program, 31

Alipirez de Leon, Julio, 166

al-Qaeda
  connection to FARC, 204
  Karzai's campaign against, 220
  links to drug trade, 216–218

American Civil Liberties Union (ACLU), 92, 102, 103, 106, 107, 235

Andean Counterdrug Initiative (ACI), of United States, 27–36

Anti-Drug Abuse Act (1986), 93

Antidrug strategy
  demand reduction, 19–21
  drug treatment courts, 24–25
  economic costs of, 69
  law enforcement, 25–26
  supply reduction, 21–23, 67–74

Arellano-Felix organization, 46

Arenas, Pedro, 194

Argentina, drug trade in, 137, 218

Arrests
  of African Americans, 96
  by Colombian troops, 181
  by DEA agents, 171
  of doctors, 122–124
  of drug traffickers, 28, 113, 188
  false/illegal arrests, 141–142
  in Guatemala, 174
  of Hodoyan, 146
  of meth producers, 118
  in Mexico, 140
  of President Fox's team, 46
  reduction of, 38
  of Richard Paey, 90
  in Sinaloa, 139–140
  by soldiers, 142, 144
  in Tulia, Texas, 76
  in U.S., statistics for, 47
  in Watauga County, 116–117
  of women, 95–96

Ashcroft, John, 171

Assassinations/assassination attempts, 139, 147, 154, 155, 156, 185, 205